Heart Essence of the Vast Expanse

Heart Essence of the Vast Expanse

Foundational Practices and the Transmission of the Longchen Nyingthig

INTRODUCED AND TRANSLATED BY

Anne Carolyn Klein

(Rigzin Drolma)

Dawn Mountain Research Institute

Foreword by Adzom Paylo Rinpoche

Preface by Tulku Thondup Rinpoche

Epilogue by Khetsun Sangpo Rinpoche

SNOW LION

Snow Lion
An imprint of Shambhala Publications, Inc.
4720 Walnut Street
Boulder, Colorado 80301
www.shambhala.com

Paperback edition published 2020.

Cover art: Robert Beer

9 8 7 6 5 4 3 2 1

First Paperback Edition
Printed in the United States of America

♾ This edition is printed on acid-free paper that meets the American National Standards Institute Z39.48 Standard.
♻ This book is printed on 30% postconsumer recycled paper.
For more information please visit www.shambhala.com.
Snow Lion is distributed worldwide by Penguin Random House, Inc., and its subsidiaries.

LIBRARY OF CONGRESS CATALOGING-IN-PUBLICATION DATA

Names: Klein, Anne C., 1947– translator, writer of introduction.
Title: Heart essence of the vast expanse: foundational practices and the transmission of the Longchen nyingthig / translated and introduced by Anne Carolyn Klein (Rigzin Drolma), Dawn Mountain Research Institute; foreword by Adzom Paylo Rinpoche; preface by Tulku Thondup Rinpoche; epilogue by Khetsun Sangpo Rinpoche.
Description: Boulder: Snow Lion, 2020. | Includes bibliographical references.
Identifiers: LCCN 2019056506 |
ISBN 9781559394994 (trade paperback). ISBN: 9781559392839 (hardcover)
Subjects: LCSH: Rdzogs-chen. | 'Jigs-med-gling-pa Rang-byung-rdo-rje, 1729 or 1730–1798.
Classification: LCC BQ7662.4 .H43 2020 | DDC 294.3420423—dc23
LC record available at https://lccn.loc.gov/2019056506

Heart Essence transmission: field of refuge

Publisher's Acknowledgment

The publisher gratefully acknowledges the generous assistance of the Hershey Family Foundation and the Gere Foundation in making possible the publication of this book.

Contents

Part Three

Prologue: *On Transmission*

The Vastness Opens

Every story of spiritual awakening is a story of transmission. Śākyamuni, in a prior life as the youth Sumedha, bowed down before the Buddha of that age, Dīpaṃkara. He was so transformed by the dual transmission of Dīpaṃkara's own presence and hearing the word "buddha" that he vowed to become a buddha himself. Moses received transmission of God's word and experienced God's blazing power in a bush; these visions still hold together a community of worship. Christ, as Word, was himself a body of transmission. St. Teresa of Avila became the bride of Christ and in this way received Christ's most intimate knowing. Rumi, the great Sufi mystic, communed endlessly with the Friend. In every instance, transmission is how the inconceivable makes itself known.

Spiritual openings like these can, in the Tibetan perspective of this book, all be appreciated as occasions of transmission, for transmission is a dynamic that is central to spiritual development, and especially to the flourishing of mystical or esoteric understanding. Rumi says that the holy ones are theatres in which the qualities of wisdom-reality are on display. That display is also a transmission. Through the ages, transmission has rained down in different streams, demonstrating again and again that the expanse of wisdom is infinitely creative.

Guru Rinpoche, the great eighth-century initiator of Tantric practice in Tibet, received transmission from Garab Dorje, the first human practitioner of Dzogchen. Garab Dorje received transmission from the Diamond Being, Vajrasattva, himself. And Vajrasattva was the first, hence the most subtle and purifyingly powerful, expression of the pristine and simple reality that is Samantabhadra, whose name means "All Good" and who is described as the primordial Buddha and source of Dzogchen transmission. Practitioners resonate with that celebration even when we do not fully understand it.

Buddhas are continuously transmitting through their presence, their gestures, and their speech and sacred scriptures, as well as through their images. Every seeker participates in the great ongoing mystery and revelation that transmission makes available. For transmission is wisdom manifesting from the unmanifest. Transmission is also how teachings move from teacher to student, across generations and across landscapes. Such teachings are not mere words, certainly, nor mere ideas, though they encompass both. Since Dzogchen teachings are experienced as expressions of and arising from reality, they are most fully communicated in the living presence of persons who embody them. These persons teach while themselves dwelling in an awareness of that reality.

Thus, transmission is a moving stream. It is not something inanimate, like a stone, not the sort of thing that is the same wherever one finds it. With transmission it matters very much from whom you receive it, and where, and how. The lineage and realization of the bestower, as well as one's own responsiveness to him or her and one's own state at the time, all have an impact on the precise nature of transmission. This is one reason why in Tibet there are so many textual transmissions of, for example, the foundational practices. All of them express very similar concepts. The differences lay not so much with words or meaning as with lineage and the precise channel of access to their blessings. Texts of transmission are treated with the same respect as living holders of transmission—never placed on the floor, stepped on, or used as furniture. One has a living and interactive relationship with them. Transmission, as we understand it here, is something alive, something with which one interacts, not another item of consumption. Thus, a rigorously traditional lama like Adzom Paylo Rinpoche allows no recording of even his most basic and exoteric teachings.

In the West, where information is increasingly a commodity for sale and where teachings are easily available through books, the internet, CDs, and videos—meaning that such teachings and information are often exchanged through transactions among strangers—it is easy to forget that traditionally, and for very important reasons, teaching happens in relationship. If you want to connect deeply with any practice, by all means find a teacher who can give the kind of transmission that by definition cannot be fully present in a book.

Still, this is a book about transmission. It arises from and participates in transmission too. The music, the ancient words, the images, all carry some part of it. You hold in your hands a text transmitted spontaneously in the eighteenth century to Rigzin Jigme Lingpa through his visionary communication with well-known figures of the eighth and fourteenth centuries: Guru Rinpoche, Vimalamitra, and Longchen Rabjam. Jigme Lingpa's text on the *Longchen Nyingthig* foundational practices is the first text translated herein. The second text is a more recent transmission from the same lineage source, a condensation of Jigme Lingpa's text by Adzom Paylo Rinpoche, who received transmission through the Adzom branch of *Heart Essence* transmission, coming through Adzom Drukpa.

Adzom Drukpa Rinpoche (1842–1924) is an important figure in this visionary transmission. Known also as Drodul Pawo Dorje and Nagtshog Rangdrol, he was the teacher of many famous Dzogchen lamas of Kathok, Dzogchen, Palyul, and Sechen monasteries. Among the best known of his illustrious students were Dzongsar Khyentse Chökyi Lodro (d. 1959), Dilgo Khyentse Rinpoche (d. 1991), the fifth Dzogchen Rinpoche, Thupten Chökyi Dorje (d. 1935), and the fourth Dodrupchen, Rigzin Tenpe Gyaltsen (d. 1961). Adzom Drukpa himself received the *Heart Essence* transmission from the famous Patrul Rinpoche, scribe of *The Words of My Perfect Teacher.*

Thus, this book contains chantable and free-verse English translations of both Jigme Lingpa's own foundational practice text, and a condensation of that classic work by Adzom Paylo Rinpoche, who is widely regarded in his homeland as an incarnation of Jigme Lingpa. This second text came about in 1999 when Adzom Rinpoche, recognizing that Western students do not always have time for the full *Heart Essence* foundational practice from Jigme Lingpa, wrote the condensed *Heart Essence* foundational practice text that is translated in the second part of this book. He often tells students by all means to practice Jigme Lingpa's text, if possible. However, rather than see students set aside the *Heart Essence* foundational practice transmission altogether due to lack of time, he offers a condensed version for more accessible usage.

Audio of these chants, both in English and Tibetan, is available for free download at www.shambhala.com/heartessence. A list of tracks is available at the back of the book.

Under the auspices of King Trisong Detsen, 108 Tibetan translators (*lotsawa*) were chosen to work with 108 Indian pandits, initiating a collaboration between lotsawas and pandits that lasted for over four hundred years. In this way they worked to establish the Dharma in a new language and culture. We are at the beginning of this process in the West today. Adzom Rinpoche holds two things important here—rhythm and meaning. His advice is to chant the practice, Tibetan style, because in that way the transmitted blessings enter more completely.

Through rhythmic chanting, the energies of body, speech, and mind are unified in contemplation. This unity is enhanced when the meaning is understood; thus, we offer the chantable English translation. Chanting in a language one understands is also part of the tradition because it is important to understand the meaning of each individual word as one recites it. The chantable English translations of both Jigme Lingpa's and Adzom Paylo's texts are distilled into the same number of syllables per line as the Tibetan. They can be practiced and sung in the traditional way, using time-honored Tibetan melodies. Thus, one can chant this English to the traditional Tibetan melody, possibly along with the recording included here,* thereby enjoying the feel of the Tibetan rhythm together with your own language.

Because the chantable versions are necessarily succinct, we have also included more expanded free-verse prose translations as a basis for study and reflection, especially when receiving oral commentary. Footnotes supportive of study accompany the free-verse translations; the chantable translations have endnotes so as to facilitate focus on the practice itself. Recognizing that readers may read closely only one of the four renditions offered here, some notes appear more than once.

No matter how they are translated, it is important to recognize that there is much more richness in these lines than is included even in the Tibetan original. This is where oral transmission comes in. If you choose to practice from these texts, let your own mind create a bridge from the more enriched meaning, gained through study and practice, to your own chanting, whether in English or Tibetan. And again, by all means seek a qualified teacher to further your understanding.

May all who are touched by this and any holy transmission experience the unimpeded and essential vastness of their own being.

Anne Carolyn Klein/Lama Rigzin Drolma
Diamond Dawn Mountain, Capitan, New Mexico, May 22, 2006
Dakini Day and Anniversary of the Great Fifth Dalai Lama

* A downloadable practice text with Tibetan and chantable English is available at www.dawnmountain.org.

Foreword

BY ADZOM PAYLO RINPOCHE

WHAT WE KNOW as *Heart Essence, the Vast Expanse* is a transmission of blessings that came about when the conqueror Longchen Rabjam's realizational mindstream welled up as a mind-treasure in the wisdom expanse, the stainless heart-mind, of omniscient Jigme Lingpa.

While harmonious with the nine stages of the vehicles, it is exceptional among them all. It is an unsurpassed and very secret path, the Clear Light Great Completeness in which all the essential paths of Sutra and Tantra are brought together. The entire threefold essentialized heart of base, path, and fruit are thus present in it.

This path itself—the profound, blessed, and fast-acting instructions of direct transmission—is twofold: It includes the entryway foundational practices and the foundation itself. These foundational practices are easy for beginners to practice as well as extremely and marvelously profound. Although dubbed with the name "foundational," because they are the entry point to Great Completeness, they are in fact the foundation itself. Therefore, by taking up with open-hearted devotion an equally open-hearted conviction that maintains the stream of Dharma, one's mind training will be fruitful. By accumulating (the collections of wisdom and merit) and purifying again and again, one achieves an unsurpassed method for instantaneously accessing the good qualities associated with attainment of the grounds and paths. Therefore, please bring these practices to completion.

Recently, because of her devotion to the Great Completeness foundational practices and the path that is the actual foundation, both of which she has completed, my own excellent student, a woman of great scholarly accomplishment, the outstanding translator Anne Klein, whose Dharma name is Rigzin Drolma, has translated and furthered it. For this I give my thanks.

At the Dharma stronghold, the great monastery of Rege,
[composed by] Paylo, who is called Adzom Tulku, on the
twenty-fifth day of the ninth [Tibetan] month [October 27, 2005],
the anniversary of Adzom Drukpa

Preface

BY TULKU THONDUP RINPOCHE

THE TEACHINGS CONTAINED in *Heart Essence, the Vast Expanse* offer the full spectrum of trainings needed for the Dzogchen path. All three divisions of Dzogchen teachings are included within it, with a special emphasis on the space and instruction divisions. Jigme Lingpa beautifully explains the meaning of the title, *Heart Essence, the Vast Expanse* (*Longchen Nyingthig*). These teachings are so called, he writes, because they are "the essence (*thig*) of the great heart (*nying chenpo*) and the space of the vast expanse (*long*)."[1] This means that the base, the path, and the fruit of Dzogchen are themselves that very spacious essence.*

In the *Heart Essence* foundational practices, we begin by turning our hearts toward Dharma by means of four mind trainings. Vividly feeling that the field of merit, the refuge tree, is present before us, we enter the door of Buddhist practice by taking Buddha, Dharma, and Sangha as our ultimate refuge. We physically and mentally bow down before the objects of refuge in order to suffuse our entire being with refuge and to dismantle from the root our most cherished ego, the source of all suffering. Then we lay the foundation for Dharma training by developing the sublime mental attitude of serving all sentient beings without any selfish thoughts.

After this, we purify all our mental, emotional, and physical misdeeds, together with their impact and habitual traces, through the force of four powers: the source of power or purification (the buddha Vajrasattva), our heartfelt

* Because the work is already so well known in English as *Heart Essence of the Vast Expanse*, this book is so titled. However, to honor Jigme Lingpa's own interpretation, we refer to it internally as *Heart Essence, the Vast Expanse.*

regret for our misdeeds, our unconditioned pledge that we will never repeat our mistakes again, and finally, the actual purification meditation. We then accumulate additional merit by offering the whole of existence, seeing it as a pure land, without any expectation of receiving anything in return.

Finally, we engage in the practice of guru yoga. Imagining ourselves as Vajrayogini, sometimes called the Great Bliss Queen, while seeing Guru Rinpoche (Padmasambhava) and his pure land in front of us, we meditate on and pray to Guru Rinpoche with seven devotional trainings. We believe in him as the embodiment of all the enlightened ones. We pray to him as the manifestation of the ultimate pure nature, the universal truth. We recognize him as the reflection of our own buddha-nature and buddha-qualities. In doing so, we open our mind with devotional energy and unite with the ultimate wisdom guru, the universal buddhahood.

Then we receive the empowerments of vajra body, speech, mind, and the full wisdom of Guru Rinpoche. In this way, we enjoy the union of appearance and emptiness, sound (or clarity) and emptiness, as well as the attainment of spontaneously present wisdom. Finally, we unite our mind with the sky-like wisdom-mind of Guru Rinpoche and remain in open presence, without concepts, over and over again.

By exhorting ourselves to do this meditation practice, one day we will have our first glimpses of the true wisdom-nature of our mind. That is the wisdom of the basis.

By meditating on the wisdom of the basis, our experiences and attainment become clear and strong. That is the wisdom of the path.

As a result of our training on the path, one day we will attain the three buddha-bodies and five buddha-wisdoms. That is the wisdom of fruition, fully enlightened buddhahood.

These foundational practices are simple, yet utterly comprehensive and complete. As Kyabje Dodrupchen Rinpoche has said again and again, "If you wish to attain buddhahood and serve all beings as your mothers, no other meditation is necessary—only this foundational practice."

The *Longchen Nyingthig*, or *Heart Essence, the Vast Expanse*, teaches the essence of buddhahood and the path by which we attain it. Realizing this essence requires that we receive its transmission through the channel of accomplished wisdom-minds, blessed forms, and sacred sounds. There are three ways in which *Longchen Nyingthig*, like most esoteric teachings of Buddhism, are transmitted to us from the primordial Buddha.

First, the ever-changing presence of ultimate wisdom in enlightened minds does not require transmission through word or form. Thus, transmission among buddhas is from wisdom-mind to wisdom-mind (*rgyal ba dgongs brgyud*). This lineage is complete in the unified and ever-whole presence of buddhahood. This transmission is not a case of one person teaching another or using words or indications. It is the spontaneous presence of the glow of self-awareness wisdom. It is Vajradhara[2] teaching without teaching to the oceans of buddha disciples, who are inseparable from himself.

Second, transmission among realized masters takes place through simple sacred symbols or gestures (*rig 'dzin brda' brgyud*). Such masters do not require explanation or elaborate formulas. Merely uttering a word or making a gesture completes this transmission and awakens the wisdom-nature.

Third, transmission through empowerments (*dbang*), texts (*lung*), and explanations (*khrid*) is for ordinary people who are ordinary trainees in the oral transmission (*gang zag snyan brgyud*). Most of us need detailed ceremonies and explanations to allow us to receive transmission, understand the meaning, and realize wisdom.

In addition to these three modes, the *Longchen Nyingthig* comes to us through the unique revelation lineage of mystical treasures (*zab mo gter brgyud*). In the eighth century, Guru Rinpoche transmitted the teachings of *Heart Essence, the Vast Expanse* to his disciples at Samye Monastery and concealed them within the mind-nature of King Trisong Detsen as a *ter* (*gter*), a hidden mystical treasure.

Later, Rigzin Jigme Lingpa (1729–98), a reincarnation of King Trisong Detsen, discovered the concealed teachings using the key of his wisdom memory. He transmitted those teachings to his disciples, who included the first Dodrupchen (1745–1821) and Jigme Gyalwe Nyugu (1765–1843). Since that time, the lineage of *Heart Essence, the Vast Expanse* has produced numerous great masters and accomplished hermits. Jigme Gyalwe Nyugu's famous student, Patrul Rinpoche, was a teacher of Adzom Drukpa, another important figure in this lineage. Many masters in this transmission even dissolved their mortal bodies amidst rays of light at death, leaving behind only their hair and twenty nails as a sign of their true attainment of buddhahood.

The soothing sound waves of devotionally chanting Jigme Lingpa's words, or other sacred treasures, unseal our rigid mind, clear the blockages of physical energies and channels, cleanse mental and physical toxicities, and purify emotional afflictions and karmic obscurations. It is a feast of blissful warmth, rousing our mind to unite with Guru Rinpoche's wisdom.

Professor Anne Klein (Lama Rigzin Drolma) has not only translated the text of the *Foundational Practices of Heart Essence, the Vast Expanse* into English but has also put them into a chantable format. This will be a great resource for filling boundless space with the vibration of the musical rhythms of prayer and invoking the hearts of many with the celebration of devotion.

If you meditate and recite the prayers of this practice, whether in Tibetan or English, with the right view and total devotion, then, as the teachings say, the buddha-nature of your mind will soon be awakened. The Tibetan words are the actual words concealed by the enlightened power of Guru Rinpoche in the wisdom-mind of Jigme Lingpa and then revealed from there. This is a very special quality of the Tibetan text. At the same time, if chanting in English inspires our minds more or helps us to understand the meaning—which is the heart of the practice—with greater ease, then it will be more beneficial for us.

Know that in whatever language you chant, whether Tibetan or English, both are equally the self-arisen waves of the ultimate nature, buddhahood. Through your chanting, the world will arise for you as a pure land of great joy. All sounds will reverberate as sounds of peace. Wherever you live will become a place of sacred pilgrimage for others. Whatever you say will be sacred sounds that inspire many. You will travel from happiness to happiness in this life and in the lives that will follow.

May the blessings of this sublime lineage of masters be in each and every letter and line of this sacred text to inspire the hearts and minds of all to enlightenment.

Tulku Thondup
Cambridge, Massachusetts, December 1, 2005
Guru Rinpoche Day and anniversary of the twelfth Karmapa
(Changjub Dorje, who was also a holder of the *Longchen Nyingthig*
and was, like Longchenpa himself, a student of Kumaradza)

Acknowledgments

I AM GRATEFUL FOR the financial and spiritual support that contributed to this project. In the summer of 1999, under the auspices of the Fetzer Foundation and the Foundation for Contemplative Mind in Society, I received an ACLS Contemplative Practice Grant to make a chantable English translation of Rigzin Jigme Lingpa's *Heart Essence* foundational practice text. In 2005, I received a Dean of Humanities Grant from Rice University to develop that manuscript into the present book. This process was then completed through a generous grant from the Ford Foundation.

My first connection to Dzogchen transmission was through Khetsun Sangpo Rinpoche, from whom I initially heard instructions on the foundational practices in 1974. I received these instructions again twenty-five years later from Adzom Paylo Rinpoche. I had the unspeakably good fortune to study and practice teachings that traditionally follow one's completion of *ngöndro*, especially the *Tri Yeshe Lama*, with both of these masters and with the late Lama Gompo Tsayden of Amdo. Those opportunities further enriched my appreciation of the foundational practices presented here.

The public teachings of His Holiness the Dalai Lama on Dzogchen and two private audiences with His Holiness in 1977 when I was just beginning to consider Dzogchen as a path continue to inspire me. Inspiration was furthered by transmission from other Dzogchen lineages: in chronological order, from the late sGa Rinpoche of Kinoor and Dehra Dun; from Dudjom Rinpoche and Chögyal Namkhai Norbu Rinpoche; and from Yongdzin Lopön Tenzin Namdak and Geshe Tenzin Wangyal Rinpoche. I owe all of them more than I can say; they have deepened my sense of the breadth and depth of Dzogchen transmissions and thus, inevitably, of their foundational practices. In addition, my fortune in studying the wisdom teachings of the

Middle Way with some of the greatest Geluk-trained scholars of their day has enhanced my appreciation of many aspects of Dzogchen teaching; for this I am especially grateful to Gyume Khensur Ngawang Lekden, the last abbot of the Tantric College of Lower Lhasa, Loseling Khensur Yeshe Tupden, Ganden Khensur Lati Rinpoche, and Loseling master Denma Lochö Rinpoche, all of whom came to the University of Virginia at the invitation of Jeffrey Hopkins and on the recommendation of His Holiness the Dalai Lama.

I am also grateful for the period of study I had with Tulku Thondup Rinpoche from 1982 to 1984 while I was a visiting lecturer and research associate in the Women's Studies and Religion Program at Harvard Divinity School and he was in Cambridge teaching Tibetan at Harvard's Center for the Study of World Religions. I especially thank Tulku for his invaluable answers to my many questions over the years since then; for his expansive writings on this tradition; and for his especially kind support regarding my rendition of Jigme Lingpa's foundational practices into English verse; and for his own translation of this text into prose in *The Dzogchen Innermost Essence Preliminary Practice*.

My heartfelt thanks go to my *bakshi*, Geshe Ngawang Wangyal, who in the late seventies was the first person to make me aware of the then-untranslated *The Words of My Perfect Teacher*. Thanks also to the great serendipity that caused my wonderful husband, Harvey B. Aronson, to meet Khetsun Rinpoche in a tea-stall in Sarnath in 1971, and then to introduce me to him in Darjeeling later in that same year.

And it is a pleasure to acknowledge another early translation of this text into English by Professor Jeffrey Hopkins (Sonam Kazi's even earlier translation was not available to me during this period). I frequently consulted both his and Tulku Thondup's renderings while preparing this version. Jeffrey's translation is widely available in *Tantric Practice in Nyingma*, in which he also translates lectures by Khetsun Rinpoche on *The Words of My Perfect Teacher* that were given at the University of Virginia in 1974 at Jeffrey's invitation. Nearly one hundred students attended these lectures; it was the largest class in the history of the Department of Religious Studies.

It was a great day when, on behalf of Snow Lion, Sidney Piburn agreed to publish this text together with its images of transmission. My grateful thanks and a bow to Dr. Susan Sopcak and Rev. Dr. Annette Jones for their generous donations of time and computer expertise in creating our initial digital versions of Jigme Lingpa's text and again to Susan for her work on the audio practice text. Natural Graphics Incorporated in Houston, under the direction of Sharon Jackson and Chip Lacy, supplied design elements used in that text. The highly skilled and gently dedicated assistance of Brian Nichols in compiling the final manuscript, English and Tibetan, has been both a pleasure and a necessity. Jermay Jamsu's clear precision in proofing the Tibetan was a vital contribution. I am grateful to Jetsun Kacho Wangmo for her beautiful chanting of the Tibetan and to Dawn Mountain Chanting Circle for the chanting in English. Great thanks to Francis Schmidt of Rice University's Shepherd School of Music for expertly arranging this for us. I dedicate this translation to the long life of my teachers, to their ongoing teaching, and to the profound world-benefiting success of all their students, so that everyone's happiness may increase.

Samantabhadra

Introduction[3]

IS THERE a paradox at work in the Dharma? We enter practice because we want something—peace, liberation, open-hearted presence. We learn that in order to obtain these we must do certain things. So we make effort. But we cannot really accomplish what we seek through effort. Effort can even be an obstacle. How is this?

We want the most profound, most penetrating, most efficacious practices, and we want them so much and so habitually that we don't always recognize what they are when we have them. Moreover, we tend to want them with our thinking minds or out of our emotional distress. Such wanting prevents us from opening to the deeper longing that makes us truly receptive to transmission.

Although this tension is natural, even inevitable, our most vibrant contact with transmission occurs neither through effort nor through narrow wanting. It comes when we receive the teachings in our body and being with a relaxed and open heart-mind. We can't actually do anything about this tricky setup. We can, however, sit with it and gradually allow a shift to take place. This shift is not simply a change of ideas, but a shift in the depths of our being. Ideas are generally froth and waves at the surface of what we are. The shift that practitioners seek affects the entire ocean of what we are. Practice is crucial for setting this shift in motion, even if practice itself cannot make it happen. For without practice, including the effortful practices with which we must typically begin our path, we hardly even know that this ocean exists.

We can look more closely at this interesting matter through noting how Dzogchen ("Great Completeness" or "Great Perfection") traditions address it. Dzogchen equates any type of thinking, or even the presence of a thought-image, with a conceptual mind, and all conceptual minds are, by definition, effortful. Such a mind, Dzogchen teachers emphasize, will never come into contact with the effortless state of liberation. Yet one must begin somehow! And in fact, one begins with the foundational practices, or *ngöndro* (*sngon 'gro*). These practices have traditionally provided entry into, and a vital foundation for, Dzogchen and other Tantric paths. Looking closely at a few elements of these practices, we find crucial clues as to how to meet this delicate situation of effortful action yielding un-effortful being—a situation that affects practitioners across a broad band of traditions.

Clues to the release of this apparent paradox can be found in the practices that are designed to melt away conception, as well as in profound stories about the transmission of those practices. The practices are what you do until you realize the story is true. Sometimes we are so focused on doing a practice "correctly" that we don't pay much attention to what created that practice in the first place and how it was transmitted, or the actual impact of that transmission on our being.

In oral and written teachings from Tibet, practice instructions typically begin with stories of how the text or instruction now being transmitted first emerged. These stories speak deeply to the entire dimension of body, mind, and energy. This is important because we are interested in discovering how we can meet the teachings with our full being rather than with our usual wanting self. In other words, how can we absorb practices into our being, rather than holding them at arm's length with our ideas of "me" and "mine"? The latter is inevitable when we wield those practices with effort. And yet, without question, at the early and middling stages of practice, effort is essential. It's not a problem we can avoid.

Still, *ngöndro,* the foundational practices, are ways to bring body, speech, or energy, and all aspects of mind into increasingly effortless harmony with the oceanic expanse central to Dzogchen teachings. This expanse is another name for reality, the heart of our being, and thus for mind-nature. Its vastness challenges the cramped and reified self-images that temporarily obstruct our view of the whole. Finitudes of any kind—the sense of being small and contained, the familiar urgent rush of business, passions, or plans—are simply conceptions. These conceptions are both cause and effect of energetic holdings in the body. The foundational practices illuminate these holdings and, in the end, lead to their dissolution into the expanse. As Khetsun Sangpo Rinpoche has said, "Like a fire that burns fuel, the mind consumes thought by working with it."

In the Tibetan traditions, teaching and practice sessions typically open with a reference, brief or extensive, to the foundational practices. Every lineage has its own variations, but the basic structure and principles of these practices are virtually identical. After an acknowledgment of one's guru or lineage and the intention to benefit all beings, the sequence usually begins with the four thoughts. These are reflections on (1) the preciousness of one's own life, (2) the fragility of life and the uncertainty of death's timing, (3) the inexorable nature of karma, and (4) the impossibility of avoiding suffering so long as ignorance holds one in samsara. In addition, there are two other contemplations: (5) the benefits of liberation compared to life in samsara and (6) the importance of a spiritual guide. These six are known as the outer foundational practices.

These six are combined with five inner practices, each of which is repeated one hundred thousand times. The first inner foundational practice is refuge. Refuge, writes Adzom Drukpa, is the cornerstone of all paths. Without it, he adds, quoting Candrakīrti, all vows come to nothing.[4] Most succinctly, refuge helps us cultivate a quality vital to the path and to human interaction in general: this is the quality of trust, the ability to fruitfully rely on someone or something other than oneself. Adzom Paylo Rinpoche once said that whereas relying on others in the context of samsara generally leads us astray, relying on the Dharma increases our good qualities.

This trusting relationship is traditionally described as open-hearted devotion. Buddha told Śāriputra that the ultimate is realized through open-hearted devotion alone.[5] This devotion is not some facile enthusiasm that runs in the face of reason; it is a deeply felt and increasingly confident relationship with the true. It begins as a kind of inspiration and finally becomes irreversible; in Dzogchen, it leads to a confidence that is utterly nondualistic. This is a rich avenue for contemplative as well as psychological exploration.

It is a unique feature of the *Heart Essence* refuge to encompass the refuges of Sutra, Tantra, and Dzogchen—that is, all nine vehicles. In the Sutra vehicles, we take refuge in the Three Jewels: the Buddha, his Teaching, and the Spiritual Community. In the first three Tantric vehicles,[6] we take refuge in the lama; we rely on the *yidam*, the enlightened being with whom we have a particularly close connection through transmission; and we make friends with the sky wisdom women, the dakinis. In Highest Yoga Tantra we rely on the channels of our own bodies, we train and cleanse our energies, and we purify the essential orbs that move through our channels. In this way we set in motion the possibility of the channels, winds, and bright orbs completing their potential to arise as the emanation, resplendent, and Sheer-form buddha-dimensions respectively.[7] In Dzogchen we take refuge in the essence, nature, and responsiveness of our own mind-nature; these are also aligned with the three buddha-dimensions. In other words, refuge is as infinitely rich as the state of realization itself.

Refuge is accompanied by the foundational practice of making bows. The different styles of such bows or prostrations can be summarized as "long" and "short." Both begin by touching facing palms to heart, crown, throat, and heart again.[8] In the long prostration one then stretches full length on the floor, arms extended; in the short prostration, one touches the ground with the "five points"—that is, the head, two hands, and two knees (the two feet already on the ground are not part of this count). Through practice this becomes a fluid motion, further animated by the rhythm of the refuge recitation.

The *bodhicitta* recitation, the third of the five practices, is repeated in order to strengthen one's intention to practice with a mind so expansive that it encompasses the welfare of all living beings.

The fourth practice is purification by means of the hundred-syllable mantra associated with the radiant white Vajrasattva. Vajrasattva, whose name means "Diamond Being," is said to have prayed that when he became enlightened, he would have a special power to relieve beings of the afflictions obstructing their enlightenment. The one hundred seed syllables of his mantra relate to the forty-two peaceful and fifty-eight wrathful deities intrinsic to our being. Vajrasattva contains them all.

The fifth practice is offering the mandala, wherein we symbolically offer up all wealth, possessions, and sense objects to the enlightened array. A special feature of the *Heart Essence* mandala practice is that one explicitly offers the three buddha-realms—the enlightened dimensions of the emanation, resplendent, and true aspects of enlightened beings—to all the buddhas. This is an opportunity, in fact, to experience the nature of reality as always offering and giving of itself. Indeed, every one of the foundational practices is an opportunity to experience some aspect of reality. Through the sheer power of repetition, our mind is naturally drawn to discover new meaning in the practice, and these discoveries are what light the way.

Another type of offering is the "beggar's accumulation of merit," an offering of the body also known, when done more elaborately, as severance, or *chöd* (*gcod*). Although not technically part of the foundational practices, it is included in the daily recitation and is a rich practice unto itself. Implicitly, all these inner foundational practices are forms of guru yoga: they all provide opportunities to unify with the enlightened mind of the buddha-guru. Explicit guru yoga is also a crucial practice. Practitioners accumulate ten million or, in some systems, thirteen rounds of one hundred thousand recitations of the vajra guru mantra.

All these practices together, and any one of them individually, flow into the view of Dzogchen. Each of the inner practices is an opportunity to allow your conceptual processes, thoughts, and visualizations to dissolve into vastness. That vastness is an effortless state; concepts and striving only obstruct it. Thus, the foundational practices absorb one's effort and transform it into effortlessness. In this way, as we have said, the foundational practices gradually reconfigure the energies of body, speech, and mind. It is a path of many blessings, a reservoir of transmissions from the earliest period of Dzogchen practice in Tibet.

Instructions for meditation are written in poetic meter and chanted aloud rhythmically. The chanted melody opens and moves currents of energy; the chanted words describe the vivid colors, poses, and ornaments of the enlightened ones present to you in meditation. You are engaged cognitively, energetically, imaginatively, and vocally.

These practices provide a point of departure from which we can step into a new space, letting go of old self-holdings. Finding that point of departure, that foundation, is what these practices are about. Literally, *ngöndro* means "that which goes before"; in Tibetan *ngön* means "before," and *dro* means "to go." So *ngöndro* is usually translated as "preliminary practices." This might sound unattractive, because most of us like to think of ourselves as sophisticated people who don't need preliminaries. It is also misleading, because it sounds like a kind of kindergarten, something you graduate from. But you never actually leave these practices behind, just as a house never moves off its foundation. You don't build a foundation and then say, "Now we'll put the house somewhere else." Every time you walk into your house, you are standing on its foundation, and every time you do a practice, you do it on this foundation.

That is why—no matter who you are—you do these practices. As Adzom Paylo Rinpoche once said, "His Holiness the Dalai Lama did them before receiving *Longchen Nyingthig* from Dilgo Khyentse Rinpoche. I'm called a *tulku*, and I did foundational practices five times before I received Dzogchen." That's what practitioners do.

In saying this, Adzom Rinpoche was addressing a student who felt inclined to bypass the foundations. At some time, we all may have that feeling of wanting to bypass the foundations. We want the house now! And we feel, quite sincerely, that we are exceptional, that our needs are very particular and our time limited, or that we have certain innate qualities or experiences that put us in a different category from other people, and so on. Who among us has not had such thoughts? This is, however, merely the pleading of ordinary, unaware mind, the mind that practice will dissolve . . . eventually.

Patrul Rinpoche famously observed that while some see Dzogchen teachings as profound, for him the foundational practices are even more profound. This point is easy to miss as we focus on attaining the "highest." Mara has many clever devices, and the belief that one can judge profundity by ordinary criteria is one of them.

Khetsun Sangpo Rinpoche beautifully details the foundational practices in a book of lectures given during his first visit to the United States in 1974. This book, *Tantric Practice in Nyingma*, briefly mentioned above, clearly describes the chants and imagined vistas of the foundational practices and tells many of the stories that traditionally accompany these teachings. The book is a commentary on *The Words of My Perfect Teacher*, the beloved classic by Patrul Rinpoche.

The practices known as foundational—and too easily dismissed by the limited self as merely preliminary—are brilliantly designed to reveal that the self that grasps or disdains them is in profound tension with the awakened state from which the practices themselves emerge and to which they can open. To attain the effortless we still have to make a very special sort of effort.

This fruitful, unavoidable tension energizes the entire path. By examining it carefully, we can see how the foundational practices, and the stories about their ultimate origin, contribute to dissolving the "problem" of the role of effort in reaching a state of effortlessness. This is analogous to the way in which understanding what we mean by "self" is an essential part of the process of understanding selflessness. Let us consider how (1) mind training, (2) the practice of Vajrasattva (which combines several elements typical of Tibetan tantric meditation), and (3) the transmission stories of Dzogchen contribute to such unfolding and to our understanding of what these traditions mean when they say we can ripen through relying on the blessings of lineage transmission.

Mind Training

Mind training focuses principally on the four thoughts that yield awareness and finally acceptance of personal impermanence. When we transcend the need to maintain our pretense of permanence, it becomes easier to become grounded in and to accept this mortal body fully. As Patrul Rinpoche wrote in *The Words of My Perfect Teacher*, "In your mother's womb, turn your mind to the Dharma. As soon as you are born, remember the Dharma of death."

Chögyam Trungpa Rinpoche said, "Ego is always wanting to achieve spirituality. It is rather like wanting to witness your own funeral." Remembering the Dharma of death, as Patrul Rinpoche suggests, is actually the opposite of wanting to attend your own funeral. It is preparation to know the vastness from which we emerge.

Life is a party on death row. Recognizing mortality means we are willing to see what is true. Seeing what is true is grounding. It brings us into the present and, eventually, into presence. It also brings us into our bodies, especially if we combine meditation on impermanence with an energetic awareness at the base of the spine. At first, the important thing about impermanence seems to be the limited time we have in this precious life. This is crucial and foundational, and yet it is not the whole story.

The teachings on impermanence concern the death of a self that never existed. Our sense of such a false and finite self, which initially is inseparable from our wish to practice, can dissolve. Understanding impermanence, Khetsun Rinpoche says, will lead you into the natural clarity of your own mind. To know impermanence is thus not only a path leading to what Dzogchen traditions speak of as "unbounded wholeness" (*thigle nyag cig*), it is also integral to that wholeness.[9]

The mind that grasps toward wholeness at the expense of "lesser" insights is profoundly mistaken, as we discover through trial and error. We begin to approach and sense the charisma of unbounded reality when the teachings begin to connect with something deeper than our usual self-state. Even at the very outset, what these practices themselves contain, like that for which they provide a foundation, is beyond expression.

Vajrasattva

In this practice, we find all the melodic, kinesthetic, and imaginative elements typical of Tantra. These elements help coalesce our energies in practice. Physically, you are seated in meditation posture. Energetically, you feel the chanting vibrate through your body, connecting you with other voices in the room or, if you are alone, with the felt memory of the melody as you heard it from your teacher or fellow practitioners. With this as a support it is easy to be wholeheartedly engaged in the contemplation. You begin by reciting:

> *ĀḤ*
> At the crown of my own head
> On white lotus and moon orbs
> From *HŪṂ*, Lama Dorje Sem:
> Brilliant white, resplendent form[10]
> Holding vajra, consort, bell.
> Protect me and purify
> These wrongs I rue and show you
> I bind, though it cost my life.[11]
> On a moon disc at your heart
> Mantra circles your heart *HŪṂ*
> Which I chant, invoking you.

As we observed earlier, Adzom Rinpoche teaches that chanting in poetic rhythm helps to bring in blessings more strongly. All the foundational practices move energy through the body; this is one element of their profundity.

Tibetans attribute the power of their practices, transmissions, and lamas to a type of energy literally known as "waves of splendor" (*byin bslab*; pronounced *jin lab,* rhymes with "pin drop"). The first syllable, *jin*, means "that which has been given or bestowed," as in "bestowed by the king." *Jin* also means "grace," or "gift," and, in some contexts, "splendor." The second syllable, *lab*, means "wave," like the waves of the ocean. Early Tibetan kings were considered to be direct descendants of the gods, and so these kings were imbued with supernatural qualities such as *jin*—pomp, splendor, and magnificence. Transmission is understood to occur through subtle flows of splendor carrying all the knowing and energetic patterning held by one awakened person to another in the process of awakening.[12] Thus, the *jin lab* that began as the splendor of kings later became, in Buddhist understanding, the waves of grace, or surges of splendor, that are the most profound gifts of lamas. This is what comes through the mind-body in practice. This is what is transmitted from teacher to student through teachings and, most explicitly, through initiations. The teacher's presence allows a full transmission of the blessings embedded in their being to be communicated. Still, the ultimate source of these blessings is reality itself, *chönyi* (*chos nyid*). In this way, blessings are reality releasing its intrinsic energy to practitioners, until they recognize the source for what it is. Put another way, practice allows one to recognize experientially that transmission emanates from the same reality to which it points.

Mind training, as we saw, emphasizes recognizing the preciousness of our human life and body. Vajrasattva is a purification practice that brings attention to the human body in a different way; it is a call to bring the blessing waves of Vajrasattva into every part of our body and being. The descending ambrosia is felt to eradicate all that obscures our own enlightened state. In the process of incorporating these purifying streams, you may discover some resistances that prevent you from fully receiving these streams of energy and thus from fully inhabiting the space of your own body energetically. These resistances, whether experienced as emotion, energy, or psychosomatic sensations, can be explored separately or addressed in the moment by breathing attentively into them, wherever you experience them.

Becoming the deity is central to all Tantric practice. Experiencing ourselves as enlightened beings, as a body of light, helps us to see our ordinary form as illusory, as empty. And the clearer its empty or illusory nature is for us, the more present and vivid is the deity we can become. Otherwise, our deity-sensibility is obstructed by our habitual sense of our own ordinariness. This is one more way in which ordinary effort, predicated on an ordinary and erroneous sense of self, cannot finally succeed. Our addiction to such effort is itself a kind of resistance to the surrender that is needed. It is not that we chide ourselves or judge ourselves poorly for holding such illusions; such resistance is inevitable while holding on to a finite self. Yet the more we are aware of it, the more easily it will dissolve, revealing the vast expanse.

In response to our request, light flows down from Vajrasattva through our crown, filling our body; it courses through every pore and corpuscle of our material being, filling our whole energy system and suffusing our entire awareness as well. In the process, our coarse material body fills with and becomes light until Vajrasattva blends inseparably with us. We glow and light up the universe, giving and receiving blessings. Then we dissolve back into radiant emptiness and are present in a different way.

There is every possibility that the combination of chanting, vivid imagination, and cognitive reflection will transform your body, energy, and mental state. At the same time, this very possibility can lure you into thinking that you need to change, rather than to see more deeply how you actually are in this moment. This deception is linked to the equally powerful notion that what you do is more important than how you are. And this in turn is reinforced by the idea that we are training our usual, thought-filled mind to "do" these practices well. The ordinary self cannot experience enlightenment any more than the ego can attend its own funeral. Practice is about finding the fire that dissolves the self. It is about finding a way to leave the illusion of self behind and still be there. Illusion vanishes when, as in the Vajrasattva practice, we dissolve into the radiant expanse, an open presence.

Again and again in the course of these practices, we dissolve into and arise from this expanse. Every such dissolution and emergence is an opportunity to learn about empty mind-space, to explore how emptiness relates to form and how unconstructed inner space relates to constructs and concepts.

Part of the genius of the tradition comes through in its instructions to repeat the foundational practices so many times that they again and again become fresh. It is not that you finish with them when you complete one hundred thousand repetitions. You do them every day, even if you are the Dalai Lama. This is a daily practice. It simply grows, especially if you are able to do some of these practices in retreat. To learn them is simple, and then they have astonishing power, an effect you could not predict based on mere intellectual knowledge of them or by superficially dipping into them.

This power doesn't come through in a single session or a single day; it has a quality of unfolding. Still, this doesn't mean that we always and only make steady progress toward the light. Bad days come over time, especially after good days. Progress is not like speeding down a one-way street, always heading in the same direction. Seasoned practitioners know this. One way to describe what occurs is that in practice we continually come up against who and what we are right now, and this is often at odds with the part of our being we are practicing to bring into manifestation. So I may sit down to become Vajrasattva, which is really an aspect that is always present within me, but as soon as I sit down, I feel whatever anger or fear is most conflated with my identity at this moment. We practice in the midst of that.

Then something else can happen—magic. Often it comes after the most terrible moments. We don't necessarily know why one or the other arises, but we do come to see that it's a process. The wisdom of these practices is that we just do them. We just do them without focusing on whether we feel like it or not, or whether it is sufficiently "advanced" for us or not. It's a practice; it's a commitment, an unbreakable connection with the transmission. You're tired, and you do it. You're too busy, and you do it. You don't feel like it, and you do it. You keep that solidity of practice there, no matter what. That is powerful.

In principle, these foundational practices are themselves sufficient. They connect us to the ultimate source, the primordial buddha known as Samantabhadra, who personifies reality just as it is. They contain elements of Sutra, Tantra, and Dzogchen, and for one who has received the appropriate identifications and insight, they themselves are Dzogchen practices. They provide us with a basis to receive mindnature instructions and create a foundation for all Dzogchen teachings such as *Tri Yeshe Lama*, the first sequence of practices bestowed upon students once they complete the foundational practices. Above all, they provide us with a way to connect directly, daily, and continuously with the living blessings, the "waves of splendor," that are the *Heart Essence*, or whatever one's lineage might be.

Transmission

The stories of how Dzogchen has been transmitted introduce in a skillful way the reality it teaches. This does not mean we understand every story literally; yet through these tales we are open to receiving a new understanding, one as yet unknown to the ordinary mind seeking those teachings.

One dimension of reality is pure radiant truth, known as the *dharmakāya*, the "true body" or "true dimension" of enlightened beings. Khetsun Rinpoche says that this dimension is like glass and that those fabulous-looking buddhas known as "resplendent dimension" or *sambhogakāya* buddhas are akin to the light streaming through that glass.

Dzogchen teachings about these dimensions and their expansive reality are communicated in one of three ways: through mind-to-mind direct transmission; through the use of symbols, including simple gestures; and through words. All these are different stages of manifestation from naked truth.

As Patrul Rinpoche puts it, from the primordial buddha Samantabhadra emerge infinite magical displays of compassion that arise as ubiquitous buddhas and their pure lands. Samantabhadra's "circle of disciples is not different from himself." This is a token of confidence for practitioners, since it indicates that enlightened reality is everywhere and cannot be lost. The ordinary mind may have forgotten it; the ordinary mind will never find it either. Practice lets our real nature consume that ordinary mind.

There are many astounding stories of transmission. Fantastic-sounding as they may seem, especially to secularized Westerners, they present a vision of wholeness that, while inexpressible, can be passionately, tangibly, and kinesthetically experienced. In *The Words of My Perfect Teacher*, Patrul Rinpoche displays this (and more) most ingeniously in relating the story of how the pith instructions of Dzogchen came into the world. Here are a few abbreviated scenes from this tale:

> Adhicitta, living in the heavenly realms, has a vision.
> All the buddhas of past, present, and future come before him and invoke Vajrasattva:
>> "You who possess the jewel of miraculous means,
>> Open the gate to all that beings desire."

Vajrasattva, who as we already know emanates directly from primordial reality, responds to this invocation just as he does in the foundational practices—light pours out from his heart. In this case, however, the light becomes a brilliant jeweled wheel offered to Sattvavajra, the lettered reflection of Vajrasattva's own name, and also a name for Vajrapani, the bodhisattva of power. It's a revelatory moment—one expression of primordial nature requesting teachings from another who equally displays it. Here, the teaching is seen less as a path to reality than as the play of reality. Practice invites us to join in the play—until we consciously and joyously participate in a playing we have never left.

Receiving this gift, Sattvavajra promises to teach. Drawing on the wisdom of all buddhas in all five pure lands, he transmits this wisdom fully, without a word, through symbols. The visionary Adhicitta, described as beloved of the gods and uniquely capable of comprehending this transmission, then becomes a symbol himself. He instantly transforms into the letter *HŪṂ*, seed syllable of enlightened beings. Emerging from the *HŪṂ* state in yet another guise, as the famous Garab Dorje, he brings these teachings into the human realm of writing and speech. In this way, the tale of Dzogchen's arrival in the human realm describes how specificity emerges from the vastness. The spontaneous arising of the teachings mirrors the effortless spontaneity of realization. Opening to the stream means releasing the effort that, perhaps, initially drew one to the path. In this way we approach Dzogchen, which in Jigme Lingpa's words has "no work of 'do this, don't do that.'"

The capacity of reality for particular expression is implicit in the tale of how the texts of this lineage came to be. *Heart Essence, the Vast Expanse*, one of the most widely renowned Dzogchen lineages, emerges from the visionary writing compiled by Jigme Lingpa. Taking his rest one evening, Jigme Lingpa's heart was heavy because he was not in Guru Rinpoche's direct presence. Praying deeply, he entered into a luminous clarity in which he, while flying over the great stupa at Boudhanath, encountered a sky woman, a dakini, who entrusted him with a wooden casket in which he found yellow scrolls and crystal beads. Swallowing these, as yet another dakini instructed him to do, he had, in Tulku Thondup's words, "the amazing experience that all the words of the *Heart Essence, the Vast Expanse* cycle together with their meanings had been awakened in his mind as if they were imprinted there." He had received a profound symbolic transmission. His further special gift was to transpose this into written words. But those words did not come to him through training and straining his ordinary mind, as happens with writers of ordinary words. These words flowed to and through him effortlessly. This is indeed how the best practitioners carry Dzogchen expression forward in time, into history, and into the minds of new practitioners.

Jigme Lingpa became extremely learned, not through study but through the visionary transformation of his practice. His luminous, voluminous writings are a testament to the power of nonconceptual vastness to express itself in words. No effort could produce, or even permit, the clarity that he experienced. Yet he practiced intensely for years before revelation came to him. In this story, he models the transition from effortful striving to artful activity.

Practicing with ease means easing away from the ordinary mind with its tightly knotted purposes. Every focus, however useful, limits us in some way. We practice in this more open way until concepts and images dissolve into a space that is limitless, offering no center on which to focus. No focus, therefore, for effort. Still, activity continues as before, fueled by wisdom and compassion instead of delusion and self-concern.

The fluid movement bringing primordial reality into expression through symbols and words also suggests the flowing movement of "waves of splendor" pouring from reality through the body and being of practitioners. The words and symbols of transmission, carrying the blessings of their source, are closer to the fire of wisdom, closer to the "original" primordial Buddha than less vibrant ordinary concepts. So long as the smoke of our effort obscures these blessings, we cannot fully appreciate the splendor that is their source and ours. Finding effortless ease means consuming these purposeful thoughts. We wait in simple awareness for the fire to consume them, thereby revealing the presence that is our nature. We respond afresh to words and symbols that have until now receded before our effortful creation of finite realities.

In 1974, in Charlottesville, Virginia, Khetsun Sangpo Rinpoche concluded his teaching on Jigme Lingpa's foundational practices by saying, "My own hope is that any among you who would like to begin these foundational practices will do so. In that case I will return and teach you the paths of Dzogchen." He did indeed return more than half a dozen times. Adzom Rinpoche likewise makes the foundational practices a requisite for the uniquely personal one-on-one pointing-out instructions, or *semtri* (*sems khrid*), through which he transmits Dzogchen. These teachers—like the *tertöns* of Tibet, like great lamas everywhere—grant students living access to the stream of transmission emanating from the primordial field. Even in a student's simple act of requesting blessings, the mind of chatter and distraction is invited to subside and so reveal what ordinary mind can never know. As Jigme Lingpa sings in his foundational practice text:

> Praying from my heart center,
> Not just mouthings, not just words,
> Bless me from your heart expanse,
> Fulfill my aspirations.
> With strong resolve that never weakens:
> Lama's heart-stream blessings be in me!
> All are from the first a pure land's fruits—
> Gods, mantras, and Sheer-form, the Dzogchen
> With no work of "do this, don't do that,"
> Radiant *rigpa*, past thought or knowing.
> May I see reality nakedly.

In rainbow space where thoughts are freed, may
Visions of bright orbs and buddhas grow—
Full *rigpa* display, resplendent lands,
Buddha beyond mind, quelled in the real.
May I gain the stable vased youth state.

Historical Note

Rigzin Jigme Lingpa's Text and the Web of Transmission

Rigzin Jigme Lingpa wrote two instructional texts (*khrid yig*), one each on the common and uncommon foundational practices (*sngon 'gro*). These are (1) *Instructions on Taking Up the Common Foundational Practices*[13] and (2) *Applied Mindfulness: Instructions on the Uncommon Foundational Practices.*[14] The *Longchen Nyingthig Ngöndro*, the first text translated here, was originally found in two places in the works of Jigme Lingpa. The first part, up through the short *chöd* (*gcod*), or severance, practice, can be found in the *Cycle of Variegated Topics on Secret Mantra: The Common and Uncommon Foundational Practices* in *Longchen Nyingthig.*[15] The guru yoga segment with four initiations is from Jigme Lingpa's *Externally Accomplished Guru Yoga: A Wish-Fulfilling Gem.*[16]

The first Dodrupchen, Jigme Thrinle Ozer (1745–1821), who was a direct student of Jigme Lingpa, compiled his teacher's works as the *The Good Path to Omniscience*, which became the first *Longchen Nyingthig* foundational practice text. Then Patrul Rinpoche wrote *The Words of My Perfect Teacher*, a commentary on this same work. Subsequently, Jamyang Khyentse Wangpo, the first Khyentse Rinpoche and himself an incarnation of Jigme Lingpa, wrote notes on this work entitled *Clarifications of the Good Path to Omniscience.*[17]

Stories of many of the great masters of the *Heart Essence* transmission are told in Tulku Thondup's wonderful book, *Masters of Meditation and Miracles*. Here we note only a few of the highlights directly related to the transmission lineage of the present translation.

Patrul Rinpoche (1808–87), the speech incarnation of Jigme Lingpa, wrote *The Words of My Perfect Teacher* after studying and training in the *Longchen Nyingthig Foundational Practices* at the feet of Jigme Gyalwe Nyugu no less than twenty-five times.[18] Renowned as much for his brilliance as for his humility, it is said that he once listened with interest as a novice monk, not knowing whom he addressed, enthusiastically expounded on *The Words of My Perfect Teacher* to its author.

Patrul Rinpoche was a teacher of Jamyang Khyentse Wangpo (1820–92), the body incarnation of Jigme Lingpa[19] and of Adzom Drukpa, who was known as "Vajra Hero, Tamer of Beings." Adzom Drukpa (1842–1924) received transmission on the *The Words of My Perfect Teacher* from Patrul Rinpoche himself. Just as Jigme Lingpa's eighteenth-century visions of Guru Rinpoche and Longchenpa gave rise to the *Longchen Nyingthig*, Adzom Drukpa's visions were instrumental in bringing that transmission into the twentieth century. One of his many illustrious students was Patrul Akunzang Shenphen Ozer of Amdo, among whose students was my own teacher, Lama Gompo Tsayden. Lama Gompo taught in California for several years in the 1980s before returning to Amdo, where he died in 1991. (In another karmic interlacing, Lama Gompo came to the United States because Khetsun Sangpo Rinpoche, then occupied with founding his Wish-Fulfilling Center in Nepal, had to turn down the invitation to visit and recommended Lama Gompo in his stead.)

Chögyal Namkhai Norbu Rinpoche, who teaches widely in the West and around the world and has written prolifically in Italian, English, and Tibetan, is recognized as the incarnation of Adzom Drukpa. As noted earlier, the late abbot of Adzom Gar in Tibet, Druktrul Rinpoche (1926–2001), was also recognized as the *tulku* of Adzom Drukpa.

A renowned contemporary of Adzom Drukpa was Jetsun Shugsep, who was also known as Jetsun Lochen (1865–1953), from whom Khetsun Sangpo Rinpoche received the *Longchen Nyingthig* transmission. She studied under Khamnyon Dharma Senge (d. 1890) and did a dark retreat under the first Trulzhig Rinpoche, Trulzhig Do-Ngag Lingpa. His incarnation, the present Trulzhig Rinpoche of Solu Khumbu, and Khetsun Sangpo of Sundarijal, Kathmandu, are the sole senior holders of this particular dark retreat transmission today.

One of Adzom Drukpa's many illustrious students was the great Dzongsar Khyentse Chökyi Lodro, himself a teacher of the renowned Dilgo Khyentse Rinpoche. Khetsun Sangpo Rinpoche received teachings from Dilgo Khyentse Rinpoche, as did Lama Gompo Tsayden and indeed as did nearly all the luminaries of this lineage today, including His Holiness the Dalai Lama. Khetsun Rinpoche is likewise devoted to his other root teacher, the late Dudjom Rinpoche, Jikdrel Yeshe Dorje,[20] and to Dudjom Rinpoche's elder son, another of Dzongsar Khyentse and Dilgo Khyentse Rinpoche's famous students, Dungsei Thinley Norbu Rinpoche. The well-known Sogyal Rinpoche was also a close student of Dilgo Khyentse Rinpoche; the Sakyong Mipham Rinpoche was his student as well.[21] And, to bring this tracing full circle, the renowned lama and filmmaker Khyentse Norbu Rinpoche, son of Dungsei Thinley Norbu, is the *tulku* of Khyentse Chökyi Lodro—who, as noted at the opening of this paragraph, was a student of Adzom Drukpa and a teacher of one of Khetsun Rinpoche's illustrious teachers. In these ways we see how the *Heart Essence* transmission itself connects many illustrious lineages and that the teachers specifically connected with the transmission embodied here are themselves connected with each other and with other luminaries of past and present.

Part One

JIGME LINGPA

Heart Essence, the Vast Expanse

BY RIGZIN JIGME LINGPA*

OPENING MEDITATIONS FROM THE ORAL TRADITION

Nine Breaths of Purification[22]

ORAL INSTRUCTIONS (KHETSUN SANGPO RINPOCHE)

To be recited upon waking, and/or to begin your meditation session.

Feel blessings in the form of white light streaming down from Padmasambhava and his retinue. Stretch out your left hand and draw the light toward your left nostril with your forefinger. Imagine you breathe only through this nostril and that the light entering through it fills your entire body, driving out all hatred. At the bottom of the breath, forcefully exhale through your right nostril, so that all hatred, in the form of a light brown snake, disappears in the far distance.

As the blessing-light continues to stream down, draw it with the index finger of your right hand toward your right nostril. Light again fills your body, this time driving out all desire in the form of a dark red rooster, which you

* These quite literal translations can be consulted when receiving oral commentary or when there is doubt about the precise meaning of the chantable English, which is the suggested version for actual practice. Following Adzom Rinpoche's wishes, we have not taken the liberty of adding extensive parenthetical material, thus seeking to preserve the traditionally necessary link between written and oral traditions.

expel with a soft breath through your left nostril until it vanishes in distant space.

With the third inhalation, feel the blessing light enter both nostrils, drawing it in with both forefingers. Feel the light descend through your left and right channels, then rise up through your central channel. With a forceful exhalation you drive out all ignorance, which departs through the crown of your head in the form of a gray pig and disappears into the distance.

Repeat three times, thereby expelling coarse, middling, and subtle forms of hatred, desire, and ignorance.

Purification of Speech[23]

OṂ ĀḤ HŪṂ
Red *RAṂ* fire having consumed my tongue,
Becomes a tri-spoked vajra* of red light, with
Vowels and consonants circling in its hollow core,
Pearl strands of the "auspicious cause" mantra of dependent arising,†
Whose light streams please buddhas and their children,‡
Returns, cleansing word blocks: Vajra speech.
I feel all speech blessings and siddhis here right now.

A Ā I Ī U Ū ṚI ṚĪ ḶI ḶĪ E AI O AU AṂ AḤ
KA KHA GA GHA ṄA
CHA CHHA JA JHA ÑA
ṬA ṬHA ḌA ḌHA ṆA
TA THA DA DHA NA
PA PHA BA BHA MA
YA RA LA VA
SHA ṢHA SA HA KṢHAḤ (*7 times*)

* Vowels, *āli,* and consonants, *kāli.*
† A reference to the mantra of dependent arising, for *rten 'grel* can also be understood as an omen, or indication, of that which will occur in dependence on what is happening now.
‡ The children of the buddhas are bodhisattvas.

YE DHARMA-HETU-PRABHAVĀ HETUṂ TEṢHAM
TATHAGATO HYABĀDAT TEṢHĀṂ CHA YO NIRODHĀ
*EVAṂ VĀDĪ MAHĀSHRAMAṆAḤ SVĀHĀ** (*7 times*)

[The Tathagata taught the causes of those (distressing) phenomena arising from causes, and he, that great practitioner of virtue, related as well their cessation (through practice of the path).][24]

* "About those (unsatisfactory) phenomena arising from causes, the Tathagata related the causes (for overcoming them, the path) and thus the Great Practitioner of Virtue related their cessation, so be it." This translation is adapted from that of Jeffrey Hopkins, who bases it on Cha-har Geshe's *Commentary on the Ye Dharma* (*Ye dharma'i 'grel pa*) in the *Collected Works of Cha-har dGe-bshes*, vol. 1 (New Delhi: Chatring Jansar Tenzin, 1973), pp. 569–74.

Guru Rinpoche

Heart Essence, the Vast Expanse:

Foundational Practices

CALLING THE LAMA

Lama, you know. Lama, you know. Lama, you know.
(*Having recited three times with great tenderness, continue*:)
From the lotus flower of faith* blooming in my heart center,
Rise forth, kind Lama, and protect me.
You alone are my refuge from the tormenting backlash
Of my own harsh actions and afflictions.
Please rest in the wheel of great bliss at my crown and be its ornament,
And kindly bring forth all my mindfulness and attentive
introspection.

* From Chogyi Dragpa's (*Chos kyi grags pa*) *Commentary*, p. 77. He notes that just as sunshine opens flowers, here the power of one's own faith opens the eight-petaled lotus of the heart (77.11–12).

THE COMMON FOUNDATIONAL PRACTICES

I. Gratitude for My Precious Life*

Right now, I am free from the eight impingements:
I'm not in any hell! Not a hungry ghost, not an animal,
Nor am I a long-lived (unaware) god!
Not a wild barbarian, nor
Erring in my view, nor has Buddha
Failed to arrive. And I am not dumb!

As a human being whose senses all function,
Who was born in a central land (where the teaching is central),
I'm not given to extreme, inexpiable action;
I'm open to those teachings!
I have these five personal endowments.

Buddha has come and has spoken the Dharma;
His teaching remains to this day, and I have entered it,
And an excellent spiritual friend has taken me on.
Thus, I have the five environmental endowments as well.

Though I've achieved this state, with all that I need,
These conditions are highly unstable;
Once this life expires,
I will encounter the world beyond.

* The following verses frame the four thoughts that turn our minds to practice: (1) appreciation of the specific qualities of a precious human life that bring freedom to practice, (2) life's impermanence, (3) karma, and (4) the suffering of cyclic existence. For further elaboration see the opening chapters of *The Words of My Perfect Teacher* or *Tantric Practice in Nyingma.*

Knowing Guru,* turn my mind to Dharma.
All-Knowing Greatness,† don't let me loose on low, errant paths.
Kind and knowing Lama, you are not other than they.‡

APPRECIATION OF THIS FORTUNATE HUMAN LIFE

If I fail to make meaningful this fortunate situation,
In the future I won't find such a basis for gaining liberation.
Once this good rebirth has consumed my merit,
After death I'll wander unfortunate realms in hard rebirths,
Not knowing right from wrong, hearing not a word of Dharma,
Meeting no spiritual friend—an enormous catastrophe.

If I just consider the numbers and levels of living beings,
Gaining a human body hardly ever occurs.
Even humans (mostly) lack Dharma and engage in misdeeds—
Those practicing Dharma are as rare as stars in sunlight.

Knowing Guru, turn my mind to Dharma.
All-Knowing Greatness, don't let me loose on low, errant pathways.
Kind and knowing Lama, you are not other [than Longchenpa
and Jigme Lingpa].

THE EIGHT CONTRARY CIRCUMSTANCES[25]

Even though I've arrived at this jeweled island of a human body,
A very foul mind in this good physical support
Is an unsuitable basis for accomplishing liberation:
Especially if (1) enthralled by demons[26] or (2) stirred by the
five poisons,
(3) Struck by bad karma or (4) diverted by laziness,

* A reference to Guru Rinpoche.

† Today we understand both Longchenpa and Jigme Lingpa as the omniscient lamas who are "all knowing." When Jigme Lingpa himself wrote these lines, he meant the phrase "all knowing" to invoke Longchenpa, and for his own students, the "Kind Lama" of the third line was Jigme Lingpa himself. Subsequent generations, including ourselves, understand the third line to refer to our own teacher.

‡ Here, "they" refers to Longchenpa and Jigme Lingpa.

(5) A slave serving others, (6) seeking protection out of fear, (7) pretending to practice, or
(8) Dull and so forth. These eight conditions are the impediments.

When these contrary conditions come forth,
Knowing Guru, turn my mind to Dharma.
All-Knowing Greatness, don't let me loose on low, errant pathways.
Kind and knowing Lama, you are not other than they.

THE EIGHT COUNTER-INCLINATIONS[27]

(1) Not discouraged with the world,
(2) Lacking the jewel of open-hearted devotion,
(3) Tied up by the lasso of desire
(4) And crude in my actions,
(5) Failing to refrain from the wrongful and defiled,
(6) A long way from caring (about the view),[28]
(7) Vows degenerated, and (8) pledges[29] torn asunder:
These are the eight strong counter-inclinations.

When such contrary conditions come forth,
Knowing Guru, turn my mind to Dharma.
All-Knowing Greatness, don't let me loose on low, errant paths.
Kind and knowing Lama, you are not other than they.

II. Impermanence

For the time being, I'm not tormented by illness or pain.
Not ruled by others, I am no slave.
This is an excellent opportunity!
I have independence.

If I squander, through idleness,
My fully fortunate human state,
Not only family, friends, and wealth
But my own cherished body
Will soon be taken

From my bed to a barren place,
Where it will be eaten by foxes, vultures, and dogs.
Then in the *bardo* I'll find great fear.

Knowing Guru, turn my mind to Dharma.
All-Knowing Greatness, don't let me loose on low, errant paths.
Kind and knowing Lama, you are not other than they.

III. Karma: Cause and Effect of Actions

Right and wrong ripens and follows me.

IV. Sufferings of Samsara

EIGHT HOT HELLS

Above all, if I am into a hell realm born, then
(1) On a hot iron ground, weapons slice my head and body to pieces,
(2) Saws gash, and (3) red hot hammers smash me.[30]
(4) I cry and choke in a sealed iron cell or (5) interior tomb;
(6) I'm impaled on red hot spears, (7) boiled in molten bronze,
(8) Utterly seared by fierce fire: these are the eight hot hells.

EIGHT COLD HELLS

On frozen peaks thick with ice and snow,
In an impassable abyss battered by blizzards,
Beaten by winds, cold and wild, there my flesh
(1) Blisters, (2) its sores open and glisten;
(3) My moans and wails rise ceaselessly
(4) With pain increasingly hard to bear;
My strength ebbs as one sick unto death.
(5) My breath comes in gasps while my teeth are chattering;
(6) My skin splits, (7) its fleshy wounds open
And then (8) crack open still more: these are the eight cold hells.

FOUR NEIGHBORING HELLS

Likewise, (1) my feet are sliced on a field of razors;
(2) A forest of swords slashes my body.
(3) I'm trapped in the mud of putrefied corpses or (4) enter endless hot ash.

TWO LESSER HELLS

Trapped in doors, pillars, stoves, or rope,
Always being used: the lesser hells.
When cause for any of these eighteen,
Strong hateful intentions comes about,
Knowing Guru, turn my mind to Dharma.
All-Knowing Greatness, don't let me loose on low, errant paths.
Kind and knowing Lama, you are not other than they.

HUNGRY GHOSTS

Similarly, in a land impoverished and unpleasant,
Even the words "food," "drink," and "enjoyment" are unknown.
Months and years pass without finding nourishment or liquid.
Hungry ghost bodies are emaciated
And barely have the strength to stand.
Miserliness causes the three types of hungry ghosts.*

ANIMALS

One eats the other, greatly fearing death;
Exhausted by servitude, muddled about what to do and what not;
Tormented by endless suffering:

* That is, those with (1) external obstructions (*phyi sgribs pa can*) such as inhabiting a world where there is no food or water; (2) internal obstructions (*nang gi sgrib pa can*) such that even if they find something to eat, their throat is too narrow for food to pass, the stomach too big to fill, or one's body is so hot with fever that the food dries up on the way down, and (3) bearing one's own obstructions, that is, carrying in the body many beings that torment oneself (*gos khur gyi sgrib pa can*). See *The Words of My Perfect Teacher,* p. 72.

The seed of that suffering is the dark ignorance in which I am
wandering right now.

Knowing Guru, turn my mind to Dharma.
All-Knowing Greatness, don't let me loose on low, errant paths.
Kind and knowing Lama, you are not other than they.

V. Recognizing One's Lapses: Relying on a Spiritual Friend

Though I've entered the path, I don't refrain from bad behavior;
I'm through Mahayana's door, yet lack a mind to help others;
I've received the four consecrations,*
Yet I fail to practice the creation and completion stages.†
Please, Lama, free me from such deviant paths.

Though I've not realized the view, I indulge in senseless behavior;‡
My meditation is distracted, yet I grind the grist of intellectual
understanding;§
My conduct is erroneous, yet I don't consider my own faults.
Please, Lama, free me from such crass practice.

Though death comes tomorrow, I grasp at home, clothing, and wealth;
Youth has flown, yet I neither reject nor grow weary of this world;
I've learned little, yet claim great accomplishment.
Please, Lama, free me from such ignorance.

* The four consecrations, or initiations (*dbang*), are: vase, secret, wisdom, and word. See the "Guru Yoga" recitation section (pp. 50–53 and 77–80) and the corresponding chapters in *Words* or *Tantric Practice*.

† Literally, "I do not practice the developing stage (*skyes rim*) or completing stage (*rdzogs rim*), for which the vase and secret *wangs* (initiations) grant permission."

‡ This can connote crude, improper, or unpredictable behavior or, alternatively, senseless babble. Chogyi Dragpa's *Commentary* simply glosses this as "not according with the cause and effect of karma." Tulku Thondup has translated it as "yet acts in a crazy manner."

§ Tulku Thondup notes that *kho yul 'ud 'gog 'thag* has been variously interpreted in commentaries as "indulging in persisting in grinding the hand-mill of (merely intellectual) understanding," as "relying on mere (intellectual) understanding" and as saying there is no difference whether the mind wanders or not, they "grind (true) experience into dust with great persistence." Literally, *'ud* means "loud noise or publicity"; *'gog* means "barren place"; *'thag* means "grinding," as in a mill; and *kho yul* means "intellectual understanding."

Though they plunge me into (harmful) circumstances, I seek bustle
and pilgrimage;
I stay in solitude, yet my mindstream goes rigid as wood;
Proclaim restraint, yet destroy neither desire nor hate:
Let me be free from the eight worldly habits.
May I soon be free from this heavy sleep,
Swiftly released from this dark prison.

With this strong calling, bring forth the guru's compassion.[31]

As if in response to this wish, the refuge tree appears in front of you. Feel that all the beings in it, especially Guru Rinpoche, return your gaze as you, leader of the chant, lead the others seated with you—mother and female relatives on your left, father and male relatives on your right, friends behind you and others in front—in chanting your promise of refuge and compassionate intent before these wise, kind beings.

THE UNCOMMON FOUNDATIONAL PRACTICES

I. Refuge[32]

Until full enlightenment,*
I seek refuge in the Three Real Jewels, [who are] the ones gone
to bliss (*sugatas*),[33]
In the three roots,[34]
In the nature of the channels, winds, and bright orbs,[35]
Which are [my] enlightenment mind,†
And in the mandala of essence, nature, and compassionate heart-
movement.‡

* Replete with all good qualities.

† The self-arisen wisdom.

‡ *thugs rjes*. The compassionate movement of outgoing energy that, with pure essence and spontaneously perfected nature, characterizes the mandala of an enlightened mind. In the Tibetan text, every line of the refuge verse ends with a Tibetan mark indicating that each line is a *terma* (*gterma*), or revealed treasure—in this case, from Jigme Lingpa's *Longchen Nyingthig* foundational practices.

II. Bodhicitta Motivation

HO
The manifold [sensory] appearances are
Like the illusion that the moon is there in water.
We wandering beings continually roam
The chain links of cyclic existence.
So they may rest easily in the basic space
Of their own clear reflecting presence,
I bring forth a mind intent on enlightenment
As I dwell in fourfold boundlessness.* (*3 times*)

III. Vajrasattva

Vajrasattva

ĀḤ
I'm in my ordinary form, and above my crown
Centered on a seat of white lotus and moon
Is *HŪṂ*,
And from it, my lama, the Diamond Being,
A resplendent dimension buddha, white and
glowing,
Holding vajra and bell while embracing Diamond Dignity
(Vajratopa).

* Often known as the four immeasurables, these are common to both southern and northern Buddhist traditions. They are: immeasurable love, immeasurable compassion, immeasurable joy, and immeasurable equanimity.

I implore you, please protect me!
Purify my defilements!
I lay them before you with heartfelt contrition;
Henceforth, I disavow them, though it cost my life.[36]

On the glowing moon at your heart
Is a letter *HŪṂ*, encircled by your mantra.
Chanting this mantra to call forth your mind
Brings clouds of ambrosia, the mind of enlightenment,
Through the pleasure-playing place of mother-father union,
Flowing downward like fine drops of camphor.
I implore you, in this way may the causes of karma, sufferings, and afflictions,
The illnesses, harmful spirits, and defilements,
As well as obstructions, faults, and infractions
Of myself and beings of all three realms be utterly purified.

OṂ BENDZRA SATTVA SAMAYA
MANU PALAYA
BENDZRA SATTVA TVENOPA
TISHTHA DRDHO ME BHAVA
SUTO [KHAYO] ME BHAVA
SUPO [KHAYO] ME BHAVA
ANU RAKTO ME BHAVA
SARVA SIDDHI ME TRAYATSHA
SARVA KARMA SU TSA ME
TSHITAM SHRI YAM KURU HUNG
HA HA HA HA HO
BHAGAVAN SARVA TATHAGATA
BENDZRA MA ME MUN TSA
*BENDZRI BHAVA MAHA SAMAYA SATTVA AH**

* Because it is the tradition to recite mantra as heard from one's teacher, this mantra is written here phonetically, in accordance with Tibetan pronunciation, not actual Sanskrit transcription. Most notably, in actual Sanskrit transcription, *vajra* is rendered *bendzra* and the Sanskrit *cha* is pronounced and written *tsa*. For the actual Sanskrit orthography and a translation of the mantra, see the Vajrasattva chapter in *Tantric Practice in Nyingma*. The *terma* version of this mantra ends with *ĀḤ HŪṂ PHAṬ*. The sutra version of the mantra here does not include these syllables.

After reciting (this mantra) as much as possible:

Protector, in my dark delusion I
Went against and violated my holy word (*samaya*);
Lama Protector, grant me refuge.
Leading holder of the vajra,
Your nature is great compassion;
Leader of beings,* I seek refuge in you.

Recite respectfully:

I openly lay bare all root and secondary violations of my holy word by body, speech, or mind. Please cleanse and purify this entire mass of defilements, obstructions, faults, failings, and stains.

Vajrasattva, smiling with delight, grants my wish, saying, "Child of good family, all your sins, obstructions, faults, and infractions are purified."

I feel Vajrasattva melt into light and dissolve into me; thereby, I too become Vajrasattva, appearing and empty, like a reflection in a mirror. The four luminous letter-clusters (*OṂ, VA JRA, SAT, and TVA*) encircling my heart-life syllable *HŪṂ* radiate light. Throughout the three realms, all environments and essence-beings are buddhafied into the very nature of the land and inhabitants known as the five Vajrasattva families.

OṂ BENDZRA SATTVA HŪṂ

Recite as many times as possible, then remain in equipoise.

IV. Mandala

OṂ ĀḤ HŪṂ
By wholeheartedly offering a million billionfold worlds—each one
Ten million lands filled with the seven treasures—
Along with my own body and resources,
May I turn the Dharma wheel

* Literally, "most significant (*gtso bo*) of all beings."

As a monarch of the universe (*cakravārtin*).

By offering the unexcelled, very blissful Richly Ornate Pure Land,
The five buddha families with their five inalienable attributes,*
Along with gift clouds of all sensory delights
Piled high beyond imagining,
May I enjoy a resplendent dimension (*sambhogakāya*) buddha-land.

By offering each and every purity, whatever is or could be,
And the youthful vase body[37]—whose ornaments are
Unceasing compassion and reality at play—
As well as pure perception of buddha-bodies and bright orbs,†
May I enjoy the true dimension (*dharmakāya*) buddha-land.

V. Severance‡: *A Beggar's Way of Accumulating Merit*[38]

PHAṬ
Throwing off body-cherishing, I defeat that god-fiend;
My mind surges into space through my Brahma-door.
Defeating the lord of death fiend, I become Tromo;[39]
The curved knife that destroys the affliction-fiend is in my right hand.
It shaves off my skull, defeating the fiend that is my own assembled form.[40]
My active left hand grabs this skull

* The inalienable, or definite, attributes are: (1) place: Richly Ornate Pure Land (*Akanishta*; *'Og min stug po bkod*); (2) teacher: Vairochana Gangchentso (*rnam snang gangs chen mtsho*); (3) retinue: tenth-ground bodhisattvas; (4) teaching: Mahayana; and (5) time: "continuous wheel of eternity" (*rtag pa rgyun gyi bskor ba*).

† Chogyi Dragpa glosses *'dzin* (to hold or to grasp) here as *ngos 'dzin*, a term spanning the gamut from recognition, to ascertainment, to distinguishing by virtue of specific characteristics (119.6). Here, I have used the term "pure perception." Adzom Drukpa's commentary on the mandala (beginning on p. 217), in his discussion of this verse on p. 222, does not specifically incorporate this phrase, yet it does mention perception being free of detailed discernment distinguishing between the Buddha to whom one offers and oneself who makes the offering (222.3–4). Here, "Buddha-bodies" translates *kāya* (*sku*); "bright orbs" translates the Tibetan term *thig le*.

‡ This practice, known as a body offering (*lus sbyin*), is an abbreviated form of the practice of "cutting attachment" (*gcod*).

And sets it on a hearth of three human heads—the three buddha-
dimensions.[41]
Therein, my corpse fills the billionfold universe.
It melts into ambrosia due to the syllables (*short*) *A* and *HŪṂ*
And is purified, increased, and transformed by the power of the three
syllables:
OṂ A HŪṂ

Repeat these as many times as you can.

PHAṬ
These offerings well satisfy my noble guests on high;
Massive merit complete, I gain the supreme and ordinary feats
(*siddhi*).
My samsaric guests below are delighted, their karmic debts cleared
away.
Harmful and obstructive beings are particularly satisfied:
Illness, harm, and interference subside into expansive space,
And negative circumstances and self-clinging are reduced to dust.
Finally, all the recipients, the offerings, and the giver as well
Dissolve into uncontrived Great Completeness. *ĀḤ*

VI. Guru Yoga

Vajrayogini

E MA HO
Spontaneously present land of my own vision,
  endlessly pure,
The fully displayed Copper-Colored Mountain,
At the center of which am I
In the fundamental form of Vajrayogini:*
One face, two hands, radiantly red, holding curved knife and skull,
Two feet, poised for dance, three eyes gazing
  at the sky.
On my crown, seated upon a thousand-petaled lotus,
Supported by sun and moon,
Is my root lama,
Source and union of all refuge
And indivisible from the Lake-Born Vajra Emanation.
Glowing white complexion tinged with red,
  youthful countenance,
Wearing a gown, religious robe, and brocaded shawl,†

* Where the original text read *gzhi lus rdo rje* ("basic body" vajra), it has been changed to read *rje btsun rdo rje* (honorific form of Dorje Naljorma or Vajrayogini) by Adzom Rinpoche. The meanings of the two terms are not dramatically different.
† Chogyi Dragpa notes that he wears the deep blue gown of a *mantrika,* the red-yellow religious robes of a monk, the kingly maroon shawl of a king, as well as the white brocade of a bodhisattva (125:7–10).

With one face, two hands, in the posture of
royal play,
Right hand holding a vajra, left, a skull-vase.
On his head he wears the folded [hat] of Pema Nyen Zhu.

Under his left arm, he holds a three-pointed staff
Secretly indicating the supreme mother-consort of bliss and
emptiness.
Dwelling in an expanse of rainbows, mounds of light, and luminous
bright orbs,
He is surrounded by an expanse beautified by five-colored lattices of
light
Wherein are the twenty-five emanations, the lord and his disciples,
Indian and Tibetan scholars, adepts and awareness-holders, personal
deities,
Dakinis, Dharma protectors, vowed ones, gathered like clouds.
See them in the great abiding sameness of clarity and emptiness.

CALLING THE LAMA: THE SEVEN-LINE PRAYER*

HŪṂ
On the northwest border of the Land of Orgyen
Upon a blooming† lotus stalk is
An adept of amazing and supreme feats (*siddhi*)
Widely known as the Lotus Born,
Encircled by dakini retinues:
I will practice as you did.
Please come and bring your waves of splendor;
Lotus Guru, bestow feats. *HŪṂ*

* The most famous invocation prayer for Padmasambhava; sung for the first time by dakinis at the moment of Padmasambhava's arising. With its several levels of meaning, it contains the essence of all teachings. See Tulku Thondup, *Enlightened Journey*, p. 146ff.
† Often translated as "pistil," which is seen when a flower opens. *Commentary* glosses this word as "blooming." See Tulku Thondup, *Enlightened Journey*, p. 176.

THE SEVEN-BRANCH PUJA

HRĪḤ
Emanating bodies as numerous as sands
Found in this land, I bow down.
Things displayed here or manifested by meditative power,
Whatever appears or could be, I present as seals of offering.
All nonvirtuous acts of my three doors
I acknowledge in the clear light Sheer-form dimension (*dharmakāya*).
In all masses of virtue that the
Two truths encompass, I rejoice.
I beseech you, please turn the Dharma wheel
Of the three vehicles, as suits students' capacities.
Until samsara is emptied I pray,
Please remain; do not pass into the beyond.
All roots of virtue gathered throughout the three times
I dedicate to the cause of great enlightenment.

CALLING THE LAMA*

With strong devotion:
Revered Guru Rinpoche,
Glorious coalescence
Of all Buddha's grace-waves,
The sole protector of every sentient being,
Without restraint I offer you
My body, resources, mind, heart, and breast.

From now until enlightenment,
Great revered one, Lotus Born,
Heed all my joy and all my pain,
Good and ill, my highs and lows.
OṂ ĀḤ HŪṂ VAJRA GURU PADMA SIDDHI HŪṂ

* Some arrangements of the text, such as Chogyi Dragpa's *Commentary*, place this prayer after the initiation; Khetsun Rinpoche and Tulku Thondup place it here.

Recite the mantra one hundred times, or repeat the above verse three times, reciting one hundred mantras after each repetition.[42]

With strong feeling stirring both mind and body, recite:

I have no other place of hope,
We now in the foul dregs of time (*kāliyuga*)
Sinking in swamps of unbearable pain.
Protect us from this, Great Guru.
Grant the four *wangs*, Blessed One.
Spark my realization, Compassionate One.
Purify the two obstructions, Powerful One.

When the time for my life has passed,
May I, in the land of the glorious mountain of Chamara*—
A land of unified emanation† that [comes forth from] my own [wisdom] vision—
Awaken (as a buddha) with the actual body of Vajrayogini,
In unity with the revered Lotus-Born One.‡

Through the play of great wisdom,
The miraculous display of bliss and emptiness,
May I become an excellent guide leading
All beings of the three realms.

Revered Lotus One, inspire me please!
I pray to you from the center of my heart.
This is not just mouthings, not just words.
Bestow blessings from your heart expanse;
May all my aspirations be accomplished.
OṂ ĀḤ HŪṂ VAJRA GURU PEMA SIDDHI HŪṂ

Repeat many times

* The abode of Guru Rinpoche.

† Khetsun Sangpo Rinpoche explains that this is a land "embodying the unification of the two truths, ultimate and conventional, emptiness and appearance" (*Tantric Practice*, p. 180). The Tibetan literally reads "land in which emanations are unified." From the *Commentary* of Chogyi Dragpa.

‡ In Tulku Thondup's recension through the Dodrupchen lineage, this verse appears here, before the lineage prayer. Both Khetsun Sangpo and Lama Gonpo place this verse after the four initiations. In consultation with Tulku Thondup, I have placed it in both places.

VII. Prayers to the Lineage Lamas

Tulku Sang Ngag, teaching in Portland, Oregon, in 1998, observed: "The Longchen Nyingthig is a lineage of faith." Jigme Lingpa received realization because of his faith in Guru Rinpoche and Longchen Rabjam. Here, we express faith in and connection with the entire stream of this transmission, beginning with the primordial Buddha, Samantabhadra, and continuing down to our own teachers. In this way we acknowledge and receive blessings from the living transmission that empowers our practice.

E MA HO
From a pure land without limit or one-sidedness
(Arises) the first buddha, the Sheer-form All-Good (Samantabhadra);
And you, the dynamic play of moon on water, resplendent dimension
Diamond Being (Vajrasattva);*
Fully defined emanation dimension, you Very Joyous Vajra (Garab
Dorje):
I pray you, bestow your blessing-waves of grace and consecration.

Treasure of the ultimate teaching, Śri Singha;
Transmitting lord of nine vehicles, Jampel Shenyen;†
Jñānasūtra and great pandit Vimala:
I pray you, show the way to liberation.

Sole ornament of this Jambu world, Lotus Born;
Loyal supreme heart children—king, student, and friend‡—
Revealer of oceanic heart-terma, honored Longchenpa;
Receiver of dakini-realm word treasures, Jigme Ling:
I pray you, grant me fruition, liberation.

* The Dzogchen tradition understands itself to have originated with the primordial buddha Samantabhadra and to have manifested forth through Vajrasattva to the first human Dzogchen practitioner, Garab Dorje, whose Sanskrit name is Prahevajra.
† Mañjuśrīmitra, who is the lord of Dzogchen, which is the peak, or ninth, of the nine vehicles (*yāna, theg pa*).
‡ The "heart children," or Dharma heirs, are the king, Trisong Detsen, the student, Vairochana (sometimes also said to be the twenty-five students of Guru Rinpoche), and the friend, his consort Yeshe Tsogyal (137:10).

Learned and practiced Kunzang Shenphen Pel;
Lotus in your hand, Gyalwe Nyugu;
[Real Mañjuśrī, *khenpo* called "Pema":
Please let the true nature show its face
And, as well, profound clear light *Nyingthig*.
Do-Ngag Ling, to you, great chariot,
Peerless root lama so very kind,
May both needs be just like that fulfilled.]*

Heroic lord of secrets, Kunzang Shenphen Pel;
Genuine Chenrezi, Gyalwe Nyugu;
Eye of Dharma, Trime Lodrö, I am at your feet;
And Dorje Ziji Tsel,† to whom the seven words flowed down,
May both needs be made spontaneously complete.‡

Rigzin Vajra Hero, Tamer of Beings;
Gyurme Dorje,§ Pema Wang-gi Gyal,¶
Jetsun Kunzang, Chime Wangmo, and
Thupten Pema Trinle,** glorious and good;
Great and holy *khenpo*, Karma Bendzra:††
May both needs be made spontaneously complete.
Rigzin Gyurme Thupten Gyatso, please,
May my practice come to completion.‡‡

* Adzom Rinpoche's tradition omits these bracketed lines and goes straight from the line ending with Gyalwe Nyugu to the line on the heroic lord of secrets (*gsang bdag dpa'o bo*).
† Jamyang Khyentse Wangpo.
‡ Both Adzom Rinpoche and Khetsun Rinpoche insert the above verse here.
§ The other son of the former Adzom Drukpa.
¶ A son of the former Adzom Drukpa and a former incarnation of Adzom Paylo Rinpoche.
** Student of Gyurme Dorje and Pema Wangyal and a root teacher of Adzom Paylo Rinpoche.
†† Along with Pema Trinle, Karma Vajra is a lineage holder and root lama of Adzom Paylo, from whom he received transmission of *Heart Essence, the Vast Expanse*.
‡‡ Adzom Rinpoche's transmission includes the above eight lines.

PRAYERFUL ASPIRATIONS FOR THIS LIFE

May I rely on my actual* vajra lamas as my eyes.
Having done whatever they instruct, never forsaking,
Their profound practices maintained with steadfastness,
May the blessing-waves of their heart-mind state flow into me.

All that is or could be, samsara and nirvana,
Are, from the first, unsurpassed pure lands, are
Perfectly ripe fruit—gods, mantras, and the true buddha dimension—
Great Completeness, free of effortful taking up this or relinquishing that,
The radiance of open presence, beyond mind-experience or mental analysis.†

May I nakedly see manifest reality
Within luminous rainbow light utterly unmarked by thought.
May visions of buddhas and essence orbs increase;
May I reach the full measure of open presence,
The dynamic display of resplendent pure lands.
May I awaken to the great extinguishment into reality, beyond mind,
And gain the youthful vase body, everlasting domain.

PRAYERFUL ASPIRATIONS FOR THE BARDO

If I fail to enter the experience of the great yoga,‡
My coarse body not liberated into the rarified realm,§
Then when my life constituents subside and
Death's clear light dawns

* Chogyi Dragpa's *Commentary* glosses this "meaningful lama" as "ultimate lama, the arising of wisdom and compassion that fulfills one's own and others' purposes" (138.14).
† *Commentary* glosses this as beyond the calm state (*gzhi gnas*) and beyond the analysis associated with hearing or thinking with respect to insight (*hlag mthong*) (140.2).
‡ *Commentary* glosses this "yoga" as the highest (*ati*) yoga, noting that "if one attains assurance (*gteng*) with respect to the meaning of the extinguishment into reality which is beyond mind, the practice of *ati* yoga, then one need not proceed to the bardo" (141.4–6).
§ *dbyings*. In other words, if I am unable to become enlightened before death by attaining the subtle sphere of a rainbow body, may I be liberated during the intermediate, or bardo, state.

As the primordially pure Sheer-form buddha-body (*dharmakāya*),
May my bardo apparitions liberate me
Into the bright, resplendent perfect buddha-form (*sambhogakāya*).
Having completed dynamic display
Of the paths of setting free and soaring forth,*
May I be freed like a child in her mother's lap.†

PRAYERFUL ASPIRATIONS FOR THE NEXT LIFE

If I fail to be freed into the original manifest ground—
The Sheer-form (*dharmakāya*) face
Not sought from other buddhas,
That great secret luminosity, peak of the supreme vehicle—
Then by relying on the supreme path consisting of
The five meditationless teachings,‡
May I wake to the five natural emanation lands.
Most especially, may I be born as the supreme heir
In the radiant Lotus Palace,
On that ground where Lord Orgyen,
Supreme leader to oceans of awareness-holders (*rigzin*),
Celebrates the very secret teaching, and once there,
May I gain inspiration
To serve the needs of endless living beings.

PRAYER FOR ACHIEVING THESE ASPIRATIONS

With blessing-waves from the oceans of awareness-holders
And through the inconceivable truth of basic space,
May I, in my free and fortunate human life, bring forth

* The two paths of Dzogchen practice: *khregs chod*, or setting free, and *thod rgal*, soaring forth. In the first, one sets free all tensions and releases the bonds of thought; in the second, one soars through vision.

† This verse contains the four stages of the path of soaring forth (*thogal*): (1) seeing reality nakedly (*chos nyid mngon sum*), (2) enrichment of visionary experience (*nyams snang gong 'phel*), (3) the full potential of open presence (*rig pa tshad phebs*), and (4) resolving, or quelling, into reality itself (*chos zad*).

‡ Liberation through experiencing, wearing, touching, seeing, and hearing (Chogyi Dragpa, 142:12–13). The preceding lines are also translated on the basis of his commentary.

The threefold interdependence,
Becoming complete, ripened, and cleansed,
And so attain buddhahood.

VIII. Initiation

This is the most important part of guru yoga. If you are busy, it is excellent to do the seven-line prayer and take initiation, even in abbreviated form.

See Guru Rinpoche vividly before you. Visualizing thus, recite slowly and in a deep voice:

Light rays stream from the letter *OṂ* sparkling like crystal between
The eyebrows of the guru.
They enter through my crown and
Purify my body's karma and the obstructions of its channels;
Vajra body blessings enter.
Receiving the vase consecration, I
Become a vessel for the birth phase;*
The seed for [my physically becoming]† a ripened awareness-holder is sown, and
The [seed[43] of] good fortune for gaining the rank of an emanation dimension buddha is placed in my mindstream.

Light rays stream from the letter *ĀḤ*, brilliant like a ruby in the guru's throat.
They enter through my throat and
Purify my speech karma and obstructions of my winds;
Vajra speech blessings enter.
Receiving the secret consecration, I
Become a vessel for chants and [mantra][44] recitation.
The seed of an awareness-holder having the power of longevity is sown, and

* *skyes rim.* "The development stage," the first of the two levels of Tantric practice, in which one cultivates the ability to clearly imagine oneself as a deity.

† *Commentary*, 143.17. Chogyi Dragpa further points out that "the mind ripens into the *dharmakāya*"; this consecration and the practice of rising forth or being born as a deity allows the body itself to ripen into a buddha emanation.

The good fortune to gain the stature of a complete resplendent dimension buddha is placed in my mindstream.

Light rays pour from the letter *HŪṂ*, the color of sky, in my guru's heart.
They enter through my heart and
Purify my mental karma and essence orb obstructers;
Vajra heart-mind blessings enter.
Receiving the wisdom primordial mind consecration, I
Become a vessel for the *caṇḍālī*[45] of bliss and emptiness.

The seed of an awareness-holder sealed [by my being indivisible from the heart and body Of my personal deity[46]] is sown, and
The good fortune to gain the stature of the Sheer-form dimension (*chöku*) is placed in my mindstream.

And now from the *HŪṂ* at my guru's heart-mind
A second letter *HŪṂ* springs forth like a shooting star.
It blends undifferentiably with my own mind and
Cleanses away actions of the All Base (*kun gzhi*) and the obstructions to my omniscience;
Primordial wisdom vajra blessings enter me.
Receiving the consecration of the ultimately indicative word, I
Become a vessel for the primordially pure Dzogchen.
The seed of an awareness-holder spontaneously accomplishing [the welfare of all[47]] is sown, and
The good fortune to attain the essential buddha dimension, the final fruit,
is placed in my mindstream.

In this way, unify recitation and meditation, then in the end take the four initiations.[48]

When the time for my life has passed,
May I, in the land of the glorious mountain of Chamara*—
A land of unified emanations that [comes forth from] my own
  [wisdom] vision—
Awaken [as a buddha] with the actual body of Vajrayogini,
Dazzlingly brilliant, in a ring of light,
In unity with the revered Lotus-Born One.†

From the lama's heart, warm red light swiftly arises. By its merely touching my heart as radiant Vajrayogini, I become a mass of red light [the size of a pea, which like a crackling spark flies to and[49]] dissolves into Guru Rinpoche's heart, mixing indivisibly with it as one taste.

Rest in that state, free of an object, thought, or expression. Then, rising from that:

PRAYERS

Precious and glorious root lama,
On the lotus seat of my heart reside.[50]
Graciously hold me with your great kindness;
Please bestow the full feats (*siddhi*) of body, speech, and mind.

Regarding the tale of my splendid lama's liberation,
May not even a moment of wrong view arise.
May I reverently see all the lama's activities as good, whereby
The lama's blessings flow well into my mind.

Through all my lives, may I be inseparable from
True lamas, and having practiced the gloriously delightful Dharma,
May I complete all good qualities of paths and grounds,
Swiftly gaining Vajradhara stature.

* The abode of Guru Rinpoche.

† In Tulku Thondup's recension through the Dodrupchen lineage, this verse is recited before the lineage prayer. Both Khetsun Sangpo and Lama Gonpo place this verse here, after the four initiations. In consultation with Tulku Thondup, I have placed it in both places.

DEDICATION PRAYERS: SHARING THE GOODNESS OF OUR PRACTICE

I.
By this good, may all beings
Complete the collections of goodness and wisdom;
From this goodness and wisdom, may there arise for them
Attainment of the two excellent buddha dimensions.

II.
Whatever virtue beings have
Through any acts that they have done, will do, or now are doing,
Just as did the All-Good [Samantabhadra, in order to reach]
the pure grounds,[51]
May they in all ways reach to the good.

III.
I am training to emulate all the virtues,
To be just like the knowing hero Mañjuśrī
And just like the All-Good Samantabhadra also.
And so [like them]
I too thoroughly dedicate all the goodness that I have.

IV.
All the majestic ones moving in the three times
Have constantly praised dedication as supreme;
So too all my own roots of virtue
I thoroughly dedicate toward goodly deeds
[leading to buddhahood].*

* That is, act in the manner of the bodhisattva Samantabhadra (not to be confused with the primordial Buddha Samantabhadra) as discussed in the *Bhadracaryapraṇidhāna-sūtra*.

Wherever I am born in every life,
May I attain the seven excellent qualities* of high birth,
Meet with Dharma as soon as I am born,
And have the freedom to be free to practice it correctly.

May I also please my excellent teachers there,
Practicing the Dharma day and night.
Having realized the teaching, may I accomplish its essential meaning.
Crossing the ocean of existence in that very life and
Thoroughly teaching the holy Dharma in samsara,
May I untiringly benefit others.
Bringing great unbiased waves of benefit to them,

May we all together and at once find buddhahood.

Colophon

This compilation of Dzogchen foundational practices entitled *Heart Essence, the Vast Expanse: Foundational Practices* was written by the great Tantric yogi Jigme Thrinle Ozer (1745–1821), who was trained through the kindness of many excellent teachers, including Jigme Lingpa, and kept his commitments with devotion. By the merit of this, may practitioners see their gurus as buddhas, whereby may they directly see the actual Kuntu Zangpo, open presence. May they become causes of unceasing benefit for endless oceans of sentient beings.

Translator's Colophon

Respectfully translated in the air and on the flat land of Houston by a grateful student in this transmission, with heartfelt thanks to Khetsun Sangpo Rinpoche and Adzom Paylo Rinpoche.

* *Commentary* lists the seven excellent qualities as: (1) long life, (2) freedom from illness, (3) a good body, (4) high family, (5) plentiful resources, (6) good fortune, and (7) great wisdom (149:5–7).

Wondrously One:

Jigme Lingpa's *Heart Essence* for Chanting

OPENING MEDITATIONS FROM THE ORAL TRADITION

Nine Breaths of Purification

ORAL INSTRUCTIONS (KHETSUN SANGPO RINPOCHE)

To be recited upon waking, and/or to begin your meditation session.

Feel blessings in the form of white light stream down from Padmasambhava and his retinue. Stretch out your left hand and draw the light toward your left nostril with your forefinger. Feel that you are breathing only through this nostril and that the light entering through it fills your entire body, driving out all hatred. At the bottom of the breath, forcefully exhale through your right nostril, so that all hatred, in the form of a light brown snake, disappears in the far distance.

As blessings continue to stream down, draw them with the index finger of your right hand toward your right nostril. Light again fills your body, this time driving out all desire in the form of a dark red rooster, which you expel with a soft breath through your left nostril until it vanishes in distant space.

With the third inhalation, feel the blessing light enter both nostrils, drawing it in with both forefingers. Feel the light descend through your left and right channels, then rise up through your central channel. With a forceful exhalation you drive out all ignorance, which departs through the crown of your head in the form of a gray pig and disappears into the distance.

Repeat three times, thereby expelling coarse, middling, and subtle forms of hatred, desire and ignorance.

Purification of Speech[52]

OṂ ĀḤ HŪṂ
Red *RAṂ* fire burns away my tongue,
Now a tri-spoked vajra of red light;
Letters,[53] inter-rising's essence there,
Wheels of pearl strands in its hollow core.
Their lights' gifts please buddhas, buddhas' heirs,[54]
Return, clear speech-blocks, yield vajra voice.
All speech blessings, *siddhis*,[55] I receive.

A Ā, I Ī, U Ū, ṚI ṚĪ, ḶI ḶĪ, E AI, O AU, AṂ AḤ[56] *(3 or 7 times)*
KA KHA GA GHA ṄA
*CHA CHHA JA JHA ÑA**
ṬA ṬHA ḌA ḌHA ṆA[57]
TA THA DA DHA NA[58]
PA PHA BA BHA MA
YA RA LA VA
SHA ṢHA SA HA KṢHAḤ† *(3 or 7 times)*

YE DHARMA-HETU-PRABHAVĀ HETUṂ TEṢHAM
TATHAGATO HYABĀDAT TEṢHĀṂ CHA YO NIRODHĀ
EVAṂ VĀDĪ MAHĀSHRAMAṆAḤ SVĀHĀ *(3 or 7 times)*

[The Tathagata taught the causes of those (distressing) phenomena arising from causes, and he, that great practitioner of virtue, related as well their cessation (through practice of the path).][59]

* In accordance with Tibetan pronunciation of Sanskrit, this line is traditionally pronounced *TSA, TSHA, DZA, DZHA, NYA.*
† Tibetans pronounce these as *SHA KHA ZA HANG KHYAH.*

Lama know. Lama know. Lama know.

From faith, an open flower in my heart,
Arise, sole refuge, my kind Lama.
Coarse deeds and failings now afflict me;
Protect me from this difficult lot.
Arise, adorn my great bliss crown's wheel.
Rouse me to be mindful and aware.[60]

THE COMMON FOUNDATIONAL PRACTICES[61]

I. Gratitude for My Precious Life[62]

I am now free from eight great hardships:
From (1) hell, (2) ghost state, and (3) animal life;
Not (4) a long-lived god,[63] nor (5) rudely wild;
No (6) wrong views, (7) buddhas gone, nor (8) tongue-tied.

I'm (1) human born, (2) with all my senses,
(3) In a central land, (4) act well, (5) with faith.
Graced by those five, and (1) Buddha's coming,
(2) That he did teach, and (3) teachings remain;

(4) I've entered these, (5) held by good teachers.
I've garnered these five, but even so,
Once this life ends, much is unstable;
I will be drawn into the next world.

Knowing Guru,[64] guide me[65] to Dharma.
All-Knowing Ones,[66] keep me from wrong paths.
Kind Lama, one with these Ones,[67] know me.

APPRECIATION OF THIS FORTUNATE HUMAN LIFE

Failing good use of my good fortune,
I'll find no base for freedom later.
Consuming merit with this fine life,
Once dead I'll roam unfortunate realms:
Not know right from wrong; hear no Dharma,
Meet no teachers—great catastrophe.

Counting the beings in other realms,
I know human life is more than rare,
And most lack the Dharma, do wrong deeds:
Full human life, rare as daytime stars.

Knowing Guru, guide me to Dharma.
All-Knowing Ones, keep me from wrong paths.
Kind Lama, one with these Ones, know me.

THE EIGHT CONTRARY CIRCUMSTANCES

If this jeweled isle, my own body
Has within it a very foul mind,
It is no base for liberation.
These contrary states: (1) a demon's thrall,
(2) The five poisons, (3) felled by bad karma,
(4) Lost to sloth (5) or a slave to others,
(6) Practice from fear or (7) as mere pretense,
(8) Dull minded and such—these eight counters.
When these contrary states do occur,

Knowing Guru, guide me to Dharma.
All-Knowing Ones, keep me from wrong paths.
Kind Lama, one with these Ones, know me.

THE EIGHT COUNTER-INCLINATIONS[68]

(1) Weak world aversion, (2) no jewel of faith,
(3) Bound by desire, or (4) crass in conduct,
(5) Loose with wrong deeds, (6) extreme disinterest,
(7) Vows in ruin, (8) pledges[69] ripped apart—
These eight strong counter-inclinations.

When these contrary states do occur,
Knowing Guru, guide me to Dharma.
All-Knowing Ones, keep me from wrong paths.
Kind Lama, one with these Ones, know me.

II. Impermanence

Just now unscathed by pain or illness,
Not ruled by others nor in their power,
A good time now of independence,
Which if I waste by being idle,
Not only family, friends, and wealth
But my own dear body soon will be
Taken from bed to a barren place—
A feast for foxes, vultures, and dogs.

Then in the *bardo*[70] I'll find great fear.
Knowing Guru, guide me to Dharma.
All-Knowing Ones, keep me from wrong paths.
Kind Lama, one with these Ones, know me.

III. Karma: Cause and Effect of Actions

Right and wrong ripens and follows me.

IV. Sufferings of Samsara

EIGHT HOT HELLS

And then once on hell's hot iron ground;
(1) Swords will slice my head and my body,
(2) Saws gash, and (3) hot molten hammers smash.
(4) I cry, choke, in sealed steel cell or (5) tombs;
(6) Hot spears impale, (7) in molten bronze boiled,
(8) Seared by fierce fire—these eight hot hells.

EIGHT COLD HELLS

On frozen peaks thick with ice and snow,
Narrow abyss, battering blizzards,
Beaten by winds cold and wild, my flesh
(1) Blisters, (2) its sores open and glisten.
(3) My moans and wails arise ceaselessly.
(4) With pain increasingly hard to bear,
My strength ebbs like one sick unto death.
(5) Breath gasps, teeth chatter, and
(6) my skin splits;
(7) Wounds open, (8) flesh tears—these eight cold hells.

FOUR NEIGHBORING HELLS

(1) A field of razors slice through my feet,
(2) A forest of swords slash my body,
(3) Caught in corpse mud, or (4) endless hot ash.

TWO LESSER HELLS

I'm trapped in doors, pillars, stoves, or rope,
Being used always—the lesser hells.
When cause for any of these eighteen
Strong hateful intentions comes about,
Knowing Guru, guide me to Dharma.
All-Knowing Ones, keep me from wrong paths.
Kind Lama, one with these Ones, know me.

HUNGRY GHOSTS

In poor, ugly lands, even the names
"Food," "drink," or "pleasure" are never heard.
Months and years pass, no food found, nor drink.
Weak body, can't stand, and greed is cause
For all the three types of hungry ghost.

ANIMALS

Each fears their death as another's meal;
Forced to serve others, blind to right, wrong;
Suffering in endless pain whose seed
Is the dark dullness in which I roam.
Knowing Guru, guide me to Dharma.
All-Knowing Ones, keep me from wrong paths.
Kind Lama, one with these Ones, know me.

V. Recognizing One's Lapses: Relying on a Spiritual Friend

I've found the path, yet curb not misdeeds;
Met Mahayana, yet help no one;
Received four *wangs*,[71] yet do not practice:
Lama, protect me from such wrong paths.
I have no view, yet chatter nonsense;[72]
Though mind unstable,[73] grind on with thought;

I pay no heed to bad behavior:
Lama, free me from such crass Dharma.
Near death, yet craving home, clothes, and wealth;
My youth gone, yet, not turned from this world;
Though little learned, I claim great knowing:
Lama, free me from such ignorance.
Though it misleads, I seek amusement;[74]
Although alone, mind stiff as a log;
Talk restraint, but desire and hate:
Lama, free me from the worldly eight.[75]
May I soon wake from this deep slumber;
May I soon flee from this dark prison.

With this strong calling, bring forth the guru's compassion.

As if in response to this wish, the refuge tree appears in front of you. Feel that all the beings in it, especially Guru Rinpoche, return your gaze as you, leader of the chant, lead the others seated with you—mother and female relatives on your left, father and male relatives on your right, friends behind you and others in front—in chanting your promise of refuge and compassionate intent before these wise, kind beings.

THE UNCOMMON FOUNDATIONAL PRACTICES[76]

I. Refuge

In Three Real Jewels, three root Bliss-Filled Ones;[77]
Channels, winds, bright orbs—this bodhi-mind;
Essence, nature, moving love mandala,
Until full bodhi,[78] I seek refuge. (*3 times*)

II. Bodhicitta Motivation

HO
Like moons in water, sights deceive us
We ever roam bound in cyclic chains.
So all may rest in their clear mind-sphere,
I raise bodhi through four boundless states.* (*3 times*)

III. Vajrasattva

ĀḤ
At the crown of my own head
On white lotus and moon orbs
From *HŪṂ*, Lama Dorje Sem:
Brilliant white, resplendent form[79]
Holding vajra, consort, bell.
Protect me and purify
These wrongs I rue and show you
I bind, though it cost my life.[80]
On a moon disc at your heart
Mantra circles your heart *HŪṂ*
Which I chant, invoking you.

From the play of *yab yum*[81] joined,
Nectar clouds of bodhi mind,
Camphor droplets descending
All my own and all others'
Deeds and wrongs—pain's real causes—
Sickness, harmers, dirt, false views,
And all stains please purify.

* Often known as the four immeasurables, these are common to both southern and northern Buddhist traditions. They are: immeasurable love, immeasurable compassion, immeasurable joy, and immeasurable equanimity.

OṂ BENDZRA SATTVA SAMAYA
MANU PALAYA
BENDZRA SATTVA TVENOPA
TISHTHA DRDHO ME BHAVA
SUTO [KHAYO] * *ME BHAVA*
SUPO [KHAYO] ME BHAVA
ANU RAKTO ME BHAVA
SARVA SIDDHI ME † *TRAYATSHA*
SARVA KARMA SU TSA ME
TSHITAM SHRI YAM KURU HUNG
HA HA HA HA HO
BHAGAVAN SARVA TATHAGATA
BENDZRA MA ME MUN TSA
BENDZRI BHAVA MAHA SAMAYA SATTVA AH ‡

After reciting (this mantra) as much as possible:

Protector,[82] in my dark delusion,
I broke and ruined pledges.
Lama, master, refuge trove,
Exalted vajra-holder,
So compassionate, supreme,
To you I go for refuge.

Recite respectfully:

I present and confess all broken pledges, main and secondary, of body, speech, and mind. Please clean away and purify my entire accumulation of sins, obstructions, faults, and infractions.

* In the Adzom lineage, the *TO* of *SUTO* is pronounced very strongly, and *KHAYO* is not pronounced. Similarly, in the next line's *SUPO*, *PO* is pronounced very strongly, and *KHAYO* is not pronounced.

† Adzom Paylo Rinpoche notes that some say *MA ME* here. Either is correct.

‡ Because it is the tradition to recite mantra as heard from one's teacher, this mantra (and all mantras in this text) is written here phonetically, in accordance with Tibetan pronunciation, not the actual Sanskrit transcription. Most notably, the Sanskrit *vajra* is here rendered *bendzra* and the Sanskrit *cha* is pronounced and written *tsa*. For the actual Sanskrit orthography and a translation of the mantra, see the Vajrasattva chapter in *Tantric Practice in Nyingma*. The terma version of this mantra ends with *HŪṂ PHAṬ*. The sutra version of the mantra here does not include these syllables.

Vajrasattva, smiling with delight, grants my wish, saying, "Child of good family, all your sins, obstructions, faults, and infractions are purified."

I feel Vajrasattva melt into light and dissolve into me; thereby, I too become Vajrasattva, appearing and empty, like a reflection in a mirror. The four luminous letter-clusters (*OṂ*, *VAJRA*, *SAT*, and *TVA*) encircle my heart-life syllable *HŪṂ* and radiate light. As this light extends through the three realms, all environments and beings are buddhafied into the very nature of the land and inhabitants known as the five Vajrasattva families.

OṂ BENDZRA SATTVA HŪṂ

Recite as many times as possible, then remain in equipoise.

IV. Mandala

OṂ ĀḤ HŪṂ
Offering a billion jewel-filled worlds—
Worlds of all divine and human wealth—
Also, my own body, resources.
May I turn the wheel as Dharma lord.[83]

Offering lands of bliss and beauty,
Fivefold[84] pure lands of five families,
Countless clouds of pleasing offerings—
May I enter Bright-form buddha lands.[85]

Offering pure worlds and vase of youth,[86]
Ceaseless love lit by the playful real,
Purely perceived buddhas and bright orbs—
May I know the Sheer-form buddha-lands.[87]

V. Severance: *A Beggar's Way of Accumulating Merit*[88]

PHAṬ
Body fondness done, god-fiend slain;
Mind soaring to space through my crown;
Death fiend slain, and I am Tromo.*
Stain-fiend slain with my right hand's knife,
Form-demon slain by smashing skull,
Left hand holds skull and takes it to
Tripod skull stove, the three *kāyas*.[89]
My corpse there, like the cosmos large,
Melts to nectar through *ĀḤ* and *HŪṂ*;
Grows pure, swells, and changes through three:
OṂ ĀḤ HŪṂ

Repeat these as many times as you can.

PHAṬ
High guests are fully satisfied,
Feast is complete, *siddhis* attained.
Low guests are sated, my debts paid;
Harmers, obstructers satisfied.
Ills, evil, blocks calmed in the sphere,
Foulness, clinging, blasted to dust
Till gift, giver, and giving are
Dzogchen nature uncontrived. *ĀḤ*

VI. Guru Yoga

E MA HO
Endless land, pure self-risen vision,
Splendid Copper Mountain fully there.
Me, Vajrayogini, at center:
One head, two hands, clear red in color,
Curved knife and skull, my three eyes skyward,
Poised to dance, standing on sun and moon.
On my crown lotus, my root lama,

* Tromo is a fierce black female deity.

One with all refuge, Lake-Born Tulku,
Red-tinged white skin, youthful, wearing gown,
Dharma robes, and fine brocaded shawl.[90]
One face, two hands, royal in bearing,
Right hand, vajra holds, skull-vase in left,
Wearing the hat of Pema[91] Nyen Zhu.
At left arm, his bliss-emptiness *yum*[92]
In her secret form, three-pointed staff.
He rides glowing rainbow-orbed expanse.
With five lights laced all round that expanse

Where the lord with twenty-five *tulkus*,
Sages from India and Tibet,
Rigzin,[93] *yidams*,[94] gods, dakinis, and
Protectors, vowed ones, gather like clouds,
Shining in one empty clarity.

THE SEVEN-LINE PRAYER

HŪṂ
Northwest Orgyen's border, there
On a blooming lotus stem:
Powers amazing and supreme,
Widely known as Lotus Born,
With dakinis all around.
I do practice as you did.
Please bring your waves of splendor
Guru, bring me *siddhis*. *HŪṂ*

THE SEVEN-BRANCH PUJA

HRĪḤ
Bowing emanated forms,
Many as sands in all worlds,
Offering you all good things
Present here or imagined.
Shining *dharmakāya* light

On all wrongs of my three doors.
I rejoice in all good deeds
Encompassed by the two truths.
Please turn the three Dharma wheels
As suits your students' learning.
Please don't pass to nirvana
Till samsara is empty.
May all goodness of all time
Cause the great enlightenment.

CALLING THE LAMA

With strong devotion:

Jetsun[95] Guru Rinpoche,
In you wondrously are one
All buddhas' love and blessings,
Sole protector of us all.

Body, goods, mind, heart, and breast,
I offer to you freely;
Please heed all my highs and lows
From now till enlightenment,
Great Jetsun Lotus Born One.
OṂ ĀḤ HŪṂ VAJRA GURU PADMA SIDDHI HŪṂ

Repeat 100 times.[96]

With strong feeling stirring both mind and body, recite:

With no other place of hope
In the dregs of time I now
Sink in swamps unbearable.
From this save me, great Guru;
Grant the four *wangs*, Blessed One.
Spark my knowing, Loving One.
Ban both barriers,[97] Powerful One.

OṂ ĀḤ HŪṂ VAJRA GURU PADMA SIDDHI HŪṂ

Recite the mantra one hundred times, or repeat the above verse three times, reciting one hundred mantras after each repetition.

Praying from my heart center,
Not just mouthings, not just words,
Bless me from your heart expanse,
Fulfill my aspirations.[98]
OṂ ĀḤ HŪṂ VAJRA GURU PADMA SIDDHI HŪṂ

Repeat many times.

VII. Prayers to the Lineage Lamas[99]

Tulku Sang Ngag, teaching in Portland, Oregon, in 1998, observed: "The Longchen Nyingthig is a lineage of faith." Jigme Lingpa received realization because of his faith in Guru Rinpoche and Longchen Rabjam. Here, we express faith in and connection with the entire stream of this transmission, beginning with the primordial Buddha, Samantabhadra, and continuing down to our own teachers. In this way we acknowledge and receive blessings from the living transmission that empowers our practice.

E MA HO
From lands unmarked by size or setting[100]
You, first buddha, Sheer-form* Kuntu Zang;[101]
Bright-form,† water's moon-play, Dorje Sem;[102]
Complete *Tulku*-Form‡ Garab Dorje:
Please, your blessings and empowerment.

Treasure of the teaching, Śri Singha;
Nine vehicles' king, Jampel Shenyen;[103]
Jñānasūtra, Panchen Vimala:
Please show the path to liberation.

* The actual dimension (*chos sku, dharmakāya*), the empty nature of buddha-mind.
† The resplendent dimension or Bright-form (*klong sku, sambhogakāya*).
‡ *Tulku* (*sprul sku, nirmanakāya*) refers to the emanation dimension.

Sole Jambu[104] world jewel, Lotus Born;
Your heart's children: king, student, and friend;[105]
Sign and treasure-giver, Longchenpa;
Khandros'[106] word-wealth holder, Jigme Ling:
Please grant me the fruit, liberation.

Learned and practiced Kunzang Shenphen Pel;
Lotus in your hand, Gyalwe Nyugu;
[Real Mañjuśrī, *khenpo* called "Pema,"
Please let my true nature show its face,
And, as well, profound clear light *Nyingthig.*
I pray you Do-Ngag Ling, great chariot,
And my kind unequalled root lama,
May both needs be just like that fulfilled.]*

Secrets' brave lord, Kunzang Shenpen Pel;
Real Chenrezi, Gyalwe Nyugu, and
Eye of Dharma, Trime Lodrö, you,
Seven-worded Dorje Ziji Tsel:[107]
May both needs spontaneously complete.†

Rigzin, Vajra Tamer of beings;
Gyurme Dorje, Pema Wang-gi Gyal,
Jetsun Kunzang, Chime Wangmo, and
Thupten Pema Trinley, glorious, good;
Holy great *khenpo*, Karma Bendzra:
May both needs spontaneously complete.
Rigzin Gyurme Thupten Gyatso, please,
May my practice come to completion.‡

* "Just like that" is poetic license for "spontaneously" (*lhun grub*). Adzom Rinpoche's tradition omits these bracketed lines and goes straight from the line ending with Gyalwe Nyugu to the next line on the secret hero (*gsang bdag dpa'o bo*).
† Both Adzom Rinpoche and Khetsun Rinpoche insert this verse here.
‡ Adzom Rinpoche's transmission includes the above eight lines.

PRAYERFUL ASPIRATIONS FOR THIS LIFE

May I reverse craving for this world,
Trust in vajra guru as my eyes;
Practice all my lama's instructions,
With strong resolve that never weakens:
Lama's heart-stream blessings be in me!

All are from the first a pure land's fruits—
Gods, mantras, and Sheer-form, the Dzogchen
With no work of "do this, don't do that,"*
Radiant *rigpa*, past thought or knowing.[108]
May I see reality nakedly.

In rainbow space where thoughts are freed, may
Visions of bright orbs and buddhas grow—
Full *rigpa* display, resplendent lands,
Buddha beyond mind, quelled in the real.
May I gain the stable vased youth state.

PRAYERFUL ASPIRATIONS FOR THE BARDO

Should I not enter that great yoga,
Coarse body not freed into the sphere,†
Then when life conditions fail, may death
Dawn as clear light, my Sheer-form all pure,‡
Bardo visions freed in resplendence,§
Complete skill to Set Free[109] and to Soar,[110]
Like a child freed in its mother's lap.

* *spang blang bya rtsol.* Literally, "nothing to be discarded or adopted."
† *dbyings.* That is, if I am unable to become enlightened before death by attaining the subtle sphere of a rainbow body, may I be liberated during the intermediate, or *bardo*, state.
‡ A reference to the *dharmakāya*. This "Sheer-form" of course, as noted earlier, has no form.
§ A reference to the resplendent dimension, or *sambhogakāya*.

PRAYERFUL ASPIRATIONS FOR THE NEXT LIFE

If not freed in the primordial
Peak of paths, great secret clear light sphere,
Sheer-form face shining forth from within,
Then through five "no-practice" buddha paths,[111]
May I find five innate[112] *tulku*[113] realms
In the glowing Lotus Palace, where
Rigzin oceans' leader, Lord Orgyen,
Honors secret teachings, may I there
Take birth as his first child, then rise forth
To meet the needs of endless beings.

PRAYER FOR ACHIEVING THESE ASPIRATIONS

With grace-waves from oceans of *rigzin,*
By the truth beyond mind, basic space,
May I, free and fortunate, bring forth
Threefold inter-risings and so be
Full, ripe, cleansed and attain buddhahood.

VIII. Initiation

This is the most important part of guru yoga. If you are busy, it is excellent to do the seven-line prayer and take initiation, even in abbreviated form.

See Guru Rinpoche vividly before you. Visualizing thus, recite slowly and in a deep voice:

Light streams from the letter *OṂ* sparkling like crystal
between the eyebrows of the guru.
They enter through my crown,
Cleansing body actions and channels;
Vajra body blessings flow.
Receiving the vase *wang*, I
Am creation phase[114] vessel;
Ripened *rigzin* seed is sown, and
The *tulku* state becomes my future.

Light streams from the letter *ĀḤ,* bright like a ruby in guru's throat.
These enter in my throat,
Cleansing my speech actions and wind blocks;
Vajra speech blessings flow.
Receiving the secret *wang*, I
Am vessel for chants;
Life-strength *rigzin* seed is sown, and
The Bright-form state becomes my future.[115]

Light streams from the sky-colored letter *HŪṂ* in guru's heart.
These enter in my heart,
Cleansing mind actions, bright orbs' blocks;
Vajra mind blessings flow.
Receiving the wisdom *wang*, I
Am vessel for bliss-empty *caṇḍālī*;[116]
Mudra rigzin seed is sown, and
The Sheer-form state becomes my future.

And now from the *HŪṂ* at the guru's heart, a second letter
HŪṂ springs forth like a shooting star,
Blends as one with my own mind,
Cleanses base acts, blocks to omniscience;
Strong wisdom blessings flow.
Receiving ultimate word *wang*, I
Am vessel for forever-pure* Dzogchen.
Right there† *rigzin* seed is sown;
Essence form,‡ the final fruit, becomes my future.

In this way, unify recitation and meditation, then in the end take the four initiations.

When my time of life has passed,
May I on great Ngayab[117] Mount,

* *Kadag*, also translated "primordially pure."
† Spontaneously perfected (*lhun grub*).
‡ Nature dimension buddha (Skt. *svabhāvikakāya,* Tib. *ngo bo nyid sku*), the unification of all three buddha dimensions, which are always attained simultaneously.

Land of unified *tulku*,
Vajrayogini body,
Sparkling clear and radiant,
One with Jetsun Pema Jung.[118]
Awakening in that state,
May I with great wisdom play,
Magic bliss, empty display,
Be guide and inspiration
For all beings in all realms:
Jetsun Pema, make it so.[119]

Praying from my heart center,
Not just mouthings, not just words,
Bless me from your heart expanse;
Fulfill my aspirations.[120]

From the lama's heart, warm red light swiftly arises. By its merely touching my radiant Vajrayogini heart, I become a mass of red light [the size of a pea, which, like a crackling spark, flies to and][121] dissolves into Guru Rinpoche's heart, mixing indivisibly with it as one taste.

Rest in that state, free of any object, thought, or expression. Then, rising from that:

PRAYERS

Precious and glorious root Lama,
In the lotus of my heart reside.
See, sustain me with your great kindness,
Bestow body, speech, and mind *siddhis*.

Without even a moment's wrong view
Of the splendid Lama's life, may I
In faith see all Lama's deeds as good,
Whereby Lama's blessings fill my mind.

Through all my lives, close to true lamas,
Practicing the glorious Dharma,
May I complete all the paths and grounds,
Gaining soon the Vajradhara state.

DEDICATION PRAYERS: SHARING THE GOODNESS OF OUR PRACTICE

I.
By this good, may all complete
Masses of good and wisdom.
So, good and wise, there arise
Their two buddha-dimensions.

II.
By whatever virtues beings have,
Through their acts past, present, and future,
Just like All-Good may they in all ways
On the pure grounds touch into the good.

III.
Just as Mañjuśrī was realized,
Just as Kuntu Zangpo was also:
To become like them in every way
I share all the goodness that I have.

IV.
By all buddhas past, present, future,
Supreme sharing has been greatly praised;
So too all my own roots of virtue
I share for the sake of kindly deeds.

Wherever I'm born in every life,
May I find the excellent seven;*
Once born, meet the Dharma right away
And be free to practice correctly.
May I please my excellent teachers
Practicing the Dharma day and night,
Achieve its deep essence, in that life
Cross over the sea of samsara.

Teach the holy Dharma everywhere,
Untiringly benefit others.
With great waves of unbiased service
May we together find buddhahood.

Colophon

This compilation of Dzogchen foundational practices known as *Heart Essence, the Vast Expanse: Foundational Practices* was set forth by the great Tantric yogi Jigme Thrinle Ozer (1745–1821), who was trained through the kindness of many excellent teachers, including Jigme Lingpa, and kept his commitments with devotion. By the merit of this, may practitioners see their gurus as buddhas, whereby may they directly see the actual Kuntu Zangpo, aware presence. May they become causes of unceasing benefit for endless oceans of sentient beings.

Translator's Colophon

Respectfully translated in the air and on the flat land of Houston by a grateful student in this transmission, with heartfelt thanks to Khetsun Sangpo Rinpoche and Adzom Paylo Rinpoche.

* *Commentary* (149:5–7) lists the seven excellent qualities as: (1) long life, (2) freedom from illness, (3) a good body, (4) high family, (5) plentiful resources, (6) good fortune, and (7) great wisdom.

Part Two

Longchen Rabjam

Spontaneous Meeting

Adzom Paylo Rinpoche and the Essence Beloved by Dakinis[122]

In eighth-century Tibet, Buddhism was dawning in the fertile Yarlung Valley, home to Tibet's earliest kings. Teachings whose time was not yet ripe were being hidden by the dakini Yeshe Tsogyal. Many of these contained instructions she had received from Guru Rinpoche when they did retreat in places to the east, like Terdrom, and in the caves of Chimphu above Samye, where Tibet's first monastery had just been built.

Chimphu is a high narrow valley crested on three sides by rocky cliffs studded with caves. Since the earliest days of Buddhism in Tibet, if not before, these caves sheltered meditators in retreat. Many wonderful images can be seen in the rocks there; the sculpted forms of buddhas and yogis are said to have emerged spontaneously through blessings brought by the great practitioners who practiced there.

Among other significant events that took place at Chimphu was the sudden death of the King Trisong Detsen's eight-year-old daughter, Hlachem Pemasel. As her mother swooned in the arms of Yeshe Tsogyal, Padmasambhava briefly revived the young girl and inscribed on her heart a vermilion letter *HRĪḤ*, telling her stricken parents that because of this she would, many lifetimes in the future, come to discover Padmasambhava's own heart-essence teachings in a transmission that would become known as the *Dakini Heart Essence*. Yeshe Tsogyal was instructed to hide these teachings away so that the princess's future incarnation would be able to discover them. Until then another lineage, the *Vimalamitra Heart Essence*, would flourish.

In the thirteenth century, Pema Ledrel Tsel revealed two volumes known as the *Dakini Heart Essence*, which included the tale of how this transmission was initially bestowed on the heart of the young princess, his former incarnation. This transmission was also held by the third Karmapa, Rangjung Dorje, and eventually by the great fourteenth-century adept Longchenpa Rabjam, who unified this transmission with the earlier *Heart Essence of Vimalamitra*. When Longchenpa arrived at Chimphu, he took to it immediately, saying, "I would rather die here than be reborn elsewhere." And in fact, after doing retreat and giving teachings at Chimphu, he did die there in 1363. One can still visit his stupa on the hillside.

In the eighteenth century, Jigme Lingpa, who was also recognized as a reincarnation of the young princess, did a three-year retreat at Belri Monastery. During the winter of 1757 he experience a series of luminous visions; in one of the most famous of these, he rode a white lion around the great stupa of Boudhanath where, with the support of many dakinis, he received the lineage now known as *Heart Essence, the Vast Expanse* (*Longchen Nyingthig*). This lineage gets its name, Khetsun Rinpoche told me, because the dakinis hold this teaching as dear as an essential drop of blood in their own heart. Two years later Jigme Lingpa undertook a second three-year retreat, this time at Chimphu where, in the famous Methog Cave, which had appeared to him during his earlier retreat, he had powerful visions of Longchen Rabjam and accepted the responsibility of preserving and spreading the teachings of Longchenpa. It was at Chimphu, in the aftermath of this retreat, that he began to compose what we now know as the *Heart Essence, the Vast Expanse* cycle.

I began practice in this lineage under Khetsun Sangpo Rinpoche in 1974, and came to love it dearly. As I was led, over the next two and a half decades, through the stream of practices in this transmission, I began to plan a pilgrimage to Tibet that would center on places sacred to Yeshe Tsogyal, Padmasambhava, and this lineage.

The trip was originally planned for October of 1995. When this date proved unworkable, we postponed it. Instead, Phyllis Pay, my co-leader on the pilgrimage, and I visited Tibet briefly in the summer of 1995 to refine our itinerary. We visited Terdrom at that time and decided that, though it had originally been in our pilgrimage plans, we would forgo it.

Our actual pilgrimage took place during Sagadawa in May of 1996. A month or so before our departure I woke up from a strong dream of

Longchenpa Rabjam and Jigme Lingpa, the first time I had dreamt of them. Perhaps it was not too surprising. I had been dreaming the trip deeply for nearly a year, exploring in history books and travel guides locations that we might visit.

After our arrival in Lhasa, our first camping excursion was planned for Chimphu, which we approached by way of Samye. On the truck that took us from Samye to Chimphu were a number of nuns from Shugseb, where my teacher Khetsun Sangpo Rinpoche had received transmission of the *Heart Essence* from Ani Lochen, the great yogini also known as Jetsun Shugsep. One young nun was wearing a button with a lama's face on it. I asked her who he was. "A very great lama who is now visiting and giving teachings at Chimphu. We have all come to hear him." She assured me that we too could meet him and told me where to find him.

We pitched our tents on a green carpet of grass by a rushing stream, its waters probably mingling with a spring higher up the mountain said to have emerged during Guru Rinpoche's first teachings there. It rained during the night, leaving a film of gleaming snow on the cliffs high above us. After breakfast, we hiked up the rise behind our meadow.

Adzom Rinpoche was staying in a small monastery about five hundred feet above where we had camped and perhaps eight hundred feet below Jigme Lingpa's Methog Cave. He was teaching the *Tri Yeshe Lama*, a major teaching text containing higher practices of the *Heart Essence, the Vast Expanse* cycle, to about two hundred fifty Tibetan yogis who were practicing in upper Chimphu. These monks and nuns descended every other day for teachings, walking in twos and threes, chanting a beautifully haunting song, a call to the lama that floated through the clear air between the upper cliffs before wafting down the valley. On alternate days newer students, monks and nuns who were staying in tents on the elevated flats near the monastery, received teachings on the foundational practices of the lineage. The eleven women in our group were the only non-Tibetans in the area.

We entered his small room, our eyes dilating after the brilliant light outside. He was attended by two monks and sat energetically at the foot of his wooden bed as he received our offering scarves. We bowed and introduced ourselves. After mentioning the various connections each of us had with practice and the *Heart Essence, the Vast Expanse*—most of us had completed the foundational practices—I asked whether we might receive instructions on mind-nature from him. These are especially precious teachings, usually given to relatively practiced students and potentially precipitating a significant turning point in understanding. His response was immediate: "Shall I speak to the whole group at once or to each of you individually?" Stunned by his generous offer, knowing he was already much occupied with teaching, we took the chance. "One by one, please," we asked.

"Yes, that's best," he responded without missing a beat, "because everyone is different. How could I say the same thing to all of you?"

And so we began. My friend, author and translator Michele Martin, and I translated. Thus, in addition to receiving our own teachings, we also saw him work with the other women. He usually began by asking a question, and would respond to the answers in ways that led each person gently, yet quite directly, by a route unique to her situation to the essence he wished to impart. He closed by giving instructions on a simple meditation practice that he felt addressed the person's situation and invited her to return the next day for further instructions.

Throughout our work with him, I continued to feel the impact of what had transpired earlier. Before the individual sessions began, and in response to our own introductions, Adzom Rinpoche had also been introduced. His attendants took it on themselves to read to us from an ornately phrased English biography which stated that three days after his birth Adzom Rinpoche began to speak "in so loving a manner that people were left in joy and astonishment." At the age of one year he was recognized by the abbot of Adzom Monastery as the incarnation of Gyalse Pema Wangyal. The attendant, who I later learned was Gyurme Tsering, then read a list of the other personages incarnated in Adzom Rinpoche. One was Trisong Detsen, father of the young princess who died at Chimphu. Another was Jigme Lingpa. On hearing this, everything holding me upright dissolved until I bent to the floor as if pushed from behind, my previously focused attention melting into a kind of spacious swoon. A few hours later, in between *semtri* translations, Rinpoche looked at me and said, "You are Rigzin Drolma." Though I had been practicing for over two decades and had taken refuge many times, this was my first Tibetan name.

Adzom Rinpoche began his studies at the age of five. Clearly an extraordinary prodigy, he undertook full-time retreat at eleven, and at his teacher's request, began teaching Dzogchen at thirteen. He is widely renowned for having left handprints in rock in Kham and has been photographed before a wooden staff he inserted into rock after a powerful ceremony. During the annual ritual known as the Great Attainment of Amitabha's Pure Land,[123] nectar has been seen (and filmed) raining down inside his monastery, with participants holding out their cups to receive it. Though he will typically respond with gentle surprise if directly asked about these things, there are many such reports.

Just before leaving Chimphu, I told Adzom Rinpoche of my dream prior to our pilgrimage. He said to me, "That dream was an indication that you would meet me." Some years later he said that a prophecy known to him had foretold our meeting.

Talking with him further, I was surprised to learn that, as a Khampa, this was only his third visit to Central Tibet. His previous visit had included a stop at Terdrom in October 1995; had we gone on our originally planned tour, we would almost surely have met him there.

Three years after our initial meeting, Rinpoche asked me if there existed a chantable version of the *Longchen Nyingthig* foundational practices. In fact, although I had said nothing of this to him, I had just completed initial work on this. In showing it to him, I asked something I had long reflected about—if it would be possible to condense this beautiful text, so that we busy Americans could participate in its transmission, a condensation that would still include the very special opening invocation to the lama and the famous refuge and bodhicitta verses from Jigme Lingpa himself. I imagined that Rinpoche would simply abbreviate the text at hand. Perhaps I underestimated how seriously he would take the needs of American students. By the next day he had created a new transmission of this ancient current of wisdom for all interested practitioners to enjoy. Placing it here alongside Jigme Lingpa's own classic text allows us to see how skillfully the central features of the older work are distilled in it.

With the kind permission of its author, this work is included here in publicly available form for the first time.

Great Bliss Blazing for Chanting

BY MIPHAM RINPOCHE[124]

Sung in Adzom Rinpoche's tradition prior to any meditation or teaching session.

OṂ ĀḤ HŪṂ HRĪḤ
Great bliss blazing power palace where
Wisdom Ones know bliss and emptiness—
Blissful lotus ones with no craving;
Vajra sun great glory shines from there.

Sheer-form[125] Amitabha; Dorje Chö;
Lokesh Lord, compassion passionate;
Lotus lord, master of world and peace;
Power Heruka outshines all things.

Sangwa Yeshe;[126] Vajravārāhī;
Demchog,[127] Desire King, great bliss treasure;
Mind-muse Rigjema[128] rules all mudras
High, low, dancing in bliss-emptiness.

Power-wielding *dak* and *daki* hosts,
You know seen and empty as the same.
You dance, your vajra form shakes three worlds;
Your laugh and ceaseless speech rouse three realms.

Red light rays suffuse all worlds and peace,
Stir and gather world, peace essences.[129]
Grant the two feats, our supreme desire:
Vajra passion of your own heart-mind.

With great vajra hooks and lassos you
Bind to great bliss all you know and see.
Dance, play in the endless magic net
Like sesame pods burst open with

Three roots, power god host, vast array.
Bless and grant as with respect I pray
For unhindered *siddhi* power in
All feats high and low that I desire.

Condensed Heart Essence:

A Close and Excellent Path to Enlightenment

BY ADZOM PAYLO RINPOCHE

From *Heart Essence, the Vast Expanse: The Condensed Foundational Practices, a Close and Excellent Path to Enlightenment*

Homage to the guru.

Nine Breathings

Oral Instructions (Adzom Paylo Rinpoche)
Inhale radiant light. Left forefinger closes left nostril. Exhale three times, first forcefully, then middling, then gently. Hatred exudes as blue-black into the distance. Repeat on the other side. Desire exudes as dark red from the left nostril. Finally, exhale three breaths through both nostrils, ignorance exudes as grey-black.

Purification of Winds

OṂ ĀḤ HŪṂ (white, red, blue) (*21 times*)

Purification of Speech

OṂ ĀḤ HŪṂ (*3 times*)

Fire rising from the syllable *RĀṂ* burns away my tongue, [which then becomes] a three-spoked vajra of red light. Circling within the periphery of its hollow core,* [looking] like a strand of pearls, are the vowels, consonants, and the heart of dependent arising [mantra].† Light radiates forth [extending] gifts that please the buddhas and their [spiritual] offspring.‡ On returning, [this light] purifies [all] speech obstructions. Thus, feel that all vajra speech blessings and *siddhis* are received.§

A Ā, I Ī, U Ū, ṚI ṚĪ, ḶI ḶĪ, E AI, O AU, AṂ AḤ¶

Radiant white, set up counterclockwise, rotate clockwise, 3 or 7 times.

KA KHA GA GHA ṄA
CHA CHHA JA JHA ÑA
ṬA ṬHA ḌA ḌHA ṆA
TA THA DA DHA NA,
PA PHA BA BHA MA
YA RA LA VA
SHA ṢHA SA HA KṢHAḤ

Red consonants, set up clockwise, rotate counterclockwise, 3 or 7 times.

YE DHARMA-HETU-PRABHAVĀ HETUṂ TEṢHAN TATHAGATO HYAVĀDAT TEṢHĀṂ CHA YO NIRODHĀ EVAṂ VĀDĪ MAHĀSHRAMAṆAḤ SVĀHĀ

Yellow letters, set up counterclockwise, rotate clockwise, 3 or 7 times.

(*Tibetan Pronunciation*: *YE DHARMĀ HETU TRABHAVĀ,*

* In other words, within its hub.

† Translation of this line accords with Adzom Rinpoche's instructions on this practice; there are variations within *Longchen Nyingthig* on how this is done. The term "dependent arising" is commonly used in colloquial language to mean an omen, a connection to, or an indication of that which will occur in the future in dependence on what is happening now.

‡ The spiritual offspring of the buddhas are bodhisattvas.

§ See note 24 in the endnotes for the extended meaning of the mantra of dependent arising.

¶ There are different methods for doing this practice; here we follow the system of the Adzom Drukpa monastery, as taught by Adzom Paylo Rinpoche.

HETUM TEKHĀM THATĀGATO HYAVADAT, TEKKHĀM TSA YO NIRODHA EWAM WĀDI MAHASHRĀMANA SOHA)

Praying to call forth the glorious Lama's heartmind:

CALLING THE LAMA

Lama know. Lama know. Lama know.
From the lotus* flower of faith that blooms in my heart center,
Rise forth, kind Lama, and protect me.
You alone are my refuge from the tormenting backlash
Of my own harsh actions and afflictions.
Please rest in the wheel of great bliss at my crown and be its ornament,
And kindly bring forth all my mindfulness and attentive introspection.

FOUR THOUGHTS TO TURN ME FROM SAMSARA

[My precious human body possessed of] freedom (*del*) and fortune (*jor*)
Is hard to find, and is deceived into meaningless distractions.
Despite impermanence and death, my enslaved mind
Is bound by its hold on permanence.
Actions and their effects are inexorable;
I fall under the power of afflictive disturbances,
My mind ensnared by samsaric suffering.

Swift sole refuge, compassionate Lama,
Transform such mind states, my kind Lama.
Let me, spurred on by knowing impermanence,
Make real meaning from this fortunate life;
Let me guard pure ethics, and so depart
This painful swirl.

* In Chogyi Dragpa's *Commentary*, he notes that just as sunshine opens flowers, here the power of one's own faith opens the eight-petaled lotus of the heart (77.11–12).

I. Refuge*

Until full enlightenment,†
I seek refuge in the Three Real Jewels, the ones gone to bliss (*sugata*);[130]
In the three roots (guru, deva, dakini);‡
In the nature of the channels, winds, and bright orbs,[131]
Which are [my] enlightenment mind;§
And in the mandala, which is essence, nature, and compassionate heart-resonance.[132]

II. Bodhicitta Motivation (*3 times*)

HO
The manifold [sensory] appearances are
Like the illusion that a moon is there in water.
We wandering beings continually roam
The chain links of cyclic existence.

So they may rest easily in the basic space
Of their own clear reflecting presence,
I bring forth a mind intent on enlightenment
As I dwell in fourfold boundlessness.¶

* This is, famously, one of the richest teaching-verses of the *ngöndro*. Numerous commentaries have been written on it with variant interpretations. The translation here accords with the commentary of Yukhok Chatralwa Choying Rangdrol (1872–1952), chosen because it also accords with the explanation from Adzom Rinpoche. Tulku Thondup's consultation was also important here.

† Replete with all good qualities.

‡ Guru, yidam (most intimate deity), and dakini.

§ Glossed as "self-arisen wisdom" (*rang 'byung ye shes*).

¶ Often known as the four immeasurables and common to both southern and northern Buddhist traditions, these are: immeasurable love, immeasurable compassion, immeasurable joy, and immeasurable equanimity.

III. Vajrasattva (*Dorje Sempa*)

ĀḤ
On a lotus and moon seat above my crown is *HŪṂ*,
From which Lama Vajrasattva [arises]: white, luminous, [with] vajra, bell,
Adorned with [the thirteen] resplendent dimension jewels and garments.
A *HŪṂ* [rests] on the moon-disc at Father-Mother's (*yab yum*) heart.
From the mantra encircling [this *HŪṂ*] descend streams of nectar
Whereby illness, [the harmful human and nonhumans known as] *dön*, as well as
Defiling faults and obstructions (blocks) are cleared away.

Recite the hundred-syllable mantra:

OṂ BENDZRA SATTVA SAMAYA
MANU PALAYA
BENDZRA SATTVA TVENOPA
TISHTHA DRDHO ME BHAVA
SUTO [KHAYO] * *ME BHAVA*
SUPO [KHAYO] ME BHAVA
ANU RAKTO ME BHAVA
SARVA SIDDHI ME † *TRAYATSHA*
SARVA KARMA SU TSA ME
TSHITAM SHRI YAM KURU HUNG
HA HA HA HA HO
BHAGAVAN SARVA TATHAGATA
BENDZRA MA ME MUN TSA
BENDZRI BHAVA MAHA SAMAYA SATTVA
ĀḤ HŪṂ, PHAṬ [133] (*21 times*)

* In the Adzom lineage, the *TO* of *SUTO* is pronounced very strongly, and *KHAYO* is not pronounced. Similarly, in the next line's *SUPO*, *PO* is pronounced very strongly, and *KHAYO* is not pronounced.

† Adzom Paylo Rinpoche notes that some say *MA ME* here; either is correct.

[Free-verse translation of the hundred-syllable mantra]

OṂ
Vajrasattva, keep [your] pledge.
Vajrasattva, reside [in me].
Make me stable, make me sated.
Fulfill me, make me compassionate.
Grant me all feats (*siddhis*) and
Make my mind virtuous in all actions.
HŪṂ HA HA HA HA HOḤ
All blessed tathagatas, do not abandon me.
Unify [with] me, great pledge being.
ĀḤ HŪṂ, PHAṬ (*21 times*)]

Vajrasattva melts into light. [This light] dissolves into me so that vessel and essence [the world and its beings] are transformed into buddhas and their pure lands.

Recite six syllables: *OṂ BENDZRA SATTVA HŪṂ* (*100 times*)

IV. Mandala

OṂ ĀḤ HŪṂ
Imagining oceans of *trikāya* pure lands
Contained in a single atom
And in each of these uncountable other [such] atoms,
I offer these to the oceans of refuge sources, whereby
May I complete the collections [of merit and wisdom]
And spontaneously bring about the ultimate benefit for both myself and others.
IDAṂ GURU RAṬNA MAṆḌALA KAṂ NIR YĀ TA YĀ MI
(I send forth this jeweled mandala to you, Precious Guru!).

V. Severance

PHAṬ
Open presence, great mother essence alight in space.
My self-grasping illusory body, and all desirable objects are laid out as feast for you,
As clouds of offerings for you, my guests!
Eat what you please, let nothing remain!
Manifest the state of the stainless *dharmakāya*.
PHAṬ[134]

VI. Guru Yoga

E MA HO
In the center of the glorious Copper-Colored Mountain,
Of my own vision, I am the very being of Vajrayogini.*
At rest on my crown, upon lotus, sun, and moon cushions
Is my lama, no different from the Lotus-Born One:
Bearing the complete symbols, objects, signs, and [resplendent dimension] adornments,
Surrounded by oceans of the Three Roots and awareness-holders (*rigzin*),
Clear in the great abiding sameness of appearance and emptiness.

HŪṂ
On the northwest border of the Land of Orgyen
Upon a blooming[135] lotus stalk is
An adept of amazing and supreme feats (*siddhis*)
Widely known as Lotus Born,
Encircled by dakini retinues.
I will practice as you did.
Please come and bring your waves of splendor;
Guru bring me *siddhis*. *HŪṂ*

* In the *Longchen Nyingthig* she appears as Yeshe Tsogyal, the Great Bliss Queen.

HRĪḤ
Respectfully I bow and make offerings,
Reveal [my] wrongdoing, and rejoice in virtue [of myself and others].
Please, turn the Dharma wheel and remain [with us] forever.
I dedicate [this] host of virtuous goodness within the radiant sphere (*dbyings*).

(*3 times*)

Great Guru, in whom all sources of refuge unite,
In my unbearable pain I yearn and from the depths of my heart call for you.
Your compassionate eyes have gazed on me;
Now please bestow blessings and the empowering consecration (*dbang*).

(*3 times, each recitation followed by one mala of this mantra:*)

OṂ ĀḤ HŪṂ BENDZRA GURU PEMA SIDDHI HŪṂ

VII. Prayers to the Lineage Lamas

E MA HO
Kunzang, Dor[je] Sem[pa],*
Garab [Dorje], Shriseng[ha],
Jampel Shenyen, Jñānasūtra and
Vima[lamitra], Lotus Born's heart children,
King, friend, and subject,
Longchen Rabjam, Rigzin Jigme Ling,
Kunzang Shenphen, Gyalwe Nyugu, and
Trime Lodrö (Patrul Rinpoche), Dorje Ziji Tsel (Jamyang Khyentse Wangpo),
Trime Longyong (Adzom Drukpa),

* Abbreviation of the Tibetan for Vajrasattva, that is, Dorje Sempa.

Gyurme Dorje,* and Pema Wangyal,†
Pema Trinle Je,‡ Karma Bendzra,§
Thupten Gyatso-la (Adzom Paylo Rinpoche),¶
To you I pray:
May the two purposes (my own and others' welfare) be spontaneously present.

A trio of light rays, white, red, and deep blue, rise in turn and [then] at once from the three syllables at [my] lama's three centers. They dissolve into my three centers in turn and then at once, whereby broken and deteriorated pledges of [my] body, speech, and mind are purified.

Waves of splendor [blessings] enter [me]. The four empowering consecrations are attained; the four obstructions (*drib*, blocks) are cleansed away; seeds of the four awareness-holders (*rigzin*) are planted.
The auspicious legacy of the four buddha-*kāya* (dimensions) are placed in the stream of [my] being.

Mixing [the guru's] heart-mind with my mind, I mentally recite [the mantra],
OṂ ĀḤ HŪṂ VAJRA GURU PADMA SIDDHI HŪṂ

The lama melts into light; (this light) dissolves into me.
Great uncontrived spontaneous presence. *ĀḤ ĀḤ ĀḤ*

Close-Lineage Prayer

I pray to awareness-holder Gyurme Dorje
And to the majestic child, Pema Wang-gi Gyal,
Together with the venerable All-Good Chime Wangmo,
May my practice come to completion.

—Written by Gyurme Dorje. Virtue.

* A son of the former Adzom Drukpa.
† The other son of the former Adzom Drukpa and the immediately previous incarnation of Adzom Paylo Rinpoche.
‡ Student of Gyurme Dorje and Pema Wangyal and a root teacher of Adzom Paylo Rinpoche.
§ Along with Pema Trinle, Karma Bendzra is a lineage holder and root lama of Adzom Paylo Rinpoche from whom he received transmission of *Heart Essence, the Vast Expanse*.
¶ Author of this abbreviated foundational practice text.

Sharing the Merit (*Three Dedication Prayers*)

Through this virtue, may I
Once having become a great guru,
Swiftly lead every wandering being without exception
To that very ground (equal to the state of the great guru I have become).

Through all successive lifetimes,
May I be inseparable from genuine lamas and
By enjoying the splendor of Dharma,
Complete all the superb qualities of the grounds and paths
And swiftly attain the state of Dorje Chang (Vajradhara).

Longchenpa, sole adornment to the beautiful teaching of the Able One (the Buddha),
Jigme Lingpa, sovereign teacher of these explanations and practices,
Until the end of existence, may we hold our peerless lamas' teachings
By hearing, thinking, and meditating on their explanations and practices.

Colophon

From the expanse of the self-arisen state of Rigzin Jigme Lingpa came forth the great path of luminous, miraculously occurring Dzogchen, this closest of paths, harmonious with all Sutric and Tantric vehicles. I myself, an ordinary person, without any bold intent to elaborate or condense his excellent and profound vajra words, am indeed embarrassed and contrite at heart because of the damage to his blessings.

Yet, in this degenerate time, due to the great force of afflictions and laziness, people find they are not up to virtue and purification, and "Something like this is necessary," said my faithful student, a great teacher at an American school, Anne Klein, whose Dharma name is Rigzin Drolma, and so forth, and who asked me again and again for the sake of many students to do this. So, in the southeastern American city of Houston, Gyurme Thupten Gyatso, called Adzom Tulku, wrote what came to his mind through the base with respect to many excellent texts of the *Heart Essence, the Vast Expanse* foundational practices.

Any faults there may be in this writing are acknowledged before the three roots. May this virtue be a cause for all beings to follow the awareness-bearing (rigzin) lama.

SARVA MANGALAṂ

Further Prayers

These can be linked with any practice session.

LONG-LIFE PRAYER FOR ADZOM GYALSE PAYLO RINPOCHE

OṂ SWASTI
By the power and blessings of the flawless[ly undeceiving] oceanic sources of refuge,
May the lotus feet of [our] teacher, powerful protector of wandering beings,
The exceedingly kind Lord of Dharma, Gyurme Thupten Gyatso,* splendid and good,
[Long and steadfastly walk among us], your exalted deeds extending everywhere.

—*Prayed by a respectful, virtuous student.*

RECITATION AFTER DEDICATION

Things, sounds, minds are gods, mantras, Sheer-forms,
Kayas and wisdom in endless play.
Through this profound and secret practice
Be one with the one taste heart-*thigle*.

Free-verse translation with distilled commentary:

[For one who knows] objects, sounds, and minds [to be] the three:
Deities, mantras, and Sheer-form buddhas (*dharmakāya*),

* His name means "Ocean of Buddha's Changeless Teachings."

The playful displays of buddha-bodies and primordial wisdom are
infinite.
Through (completing) this profound and secret yogic practice,
May we know the indivisible heart-*thigle* of one taste.

PRAYER TO THE *HEART ESSENCE* (*NYINGTHIG*) PROTECTORS

Ekazati

HŪṂ
To glorious Ekazati and
To the rishi [mountain yogi] Rahula,
the pervasive one,*
To commitment-holder Dorje Legpa
(Vajra Sadhu) and so forth,
To the teachings' hosts of protectors, to friends
of the *Heart Essence,*
I offer pledge substances consisting of tormas made of nectar.
Please protect and give refuge to this yogi, myself;
Undistractedly accomplish the activities entrusted to you.

* In traditional India, an epithet of Vishnu.

I make this virtuous offering in accordance with the heart request of Lama Shenphen from Ma Gom.

FAITHFUL STUDENT SONG

Advice Exhorting Students to Turn from Samsara, an Excellent Path to Liberation

With painful heart[-felt longing]
I call to the precious Three Jewels.
Please turn your compassionate gaze upon me!
I have no other place of hope.

The human body is difficult to attain.
When impermanence suddenly descends,
Will you be full of confidence in the face of death,
Faithful, fortunate student?

The collection of five aggregates,
The fivefold composite [of elements],
Eventually becomes unreliable.
From [the depths of] your heart, reflect on death,
Faithful, fortunate student.

Actions (karma) unfailingly bear fruit;
Give up thoughts that are nonvirtuous and
Make effort at the holy teaching,
Faithful, fortunate student.

Samsara's swirl of magical illusions ensnares and deceives;
Let your thoughts and mind be without attachment.
Escape right now [through] the path to liberation,
Faithful, fortunate student.

When your mind is not two-pointed
And your devotion irreversible,
Lama and student walk together,
Faithful, fortunate student.

Gyurme Thupten Gyatso (Ocean of Buddha's Unchanging Teaching),
To wish for [and accept] you as [our] lama from [the depths] of our hearts—
No pith instructions surpass that!
Faithful, fortunate student.

Please keep this heart-advice in your heart.
A HO A LA LA HO! Playfully and with delight I offer this most pleasing song.
A HO A LA LA HO! Playfully and with delight I offer this most pleasing song.

Waves of Splendor:

Adzom Rinpoche's *Condensed Heart Essence* for Chanting

Homage to the guru.

Nine Breathings

Oral Instructions (Adzom Paylo Rinpoche)

Inhale radiant light. Left forefinger closes left nostril. Exhale three times, first forcefully, then middling, then gently. Hatred exudes as blue-black into the distance. Repeat this for the other side. Desire exudes as dark red from the left nostril. Finally, three breaths through both nostrils; ignorance exudes as grey-black.

Purification of Winds

OṂ ĀḤ HŪṂ (white, red, blue) (*21 times*)

Purification of Speech

OṂ ĀḤ HŪṂ (*3 times*)
Red *RĀṂ* fire burns away my tongue
Now a tri-spoked vajra of red light;
Letters,[136] inter-rising's essence[137] there,
Wheels of pearl strands in its hollow core.

Their lights' gifts please buddhas, buddhas' heirs,
Return, clear speech-blocks, yield vajra voice.
All speech blessings, *siddhis*, I receive.

A Ā, I Ī, U Ū, ṚI ṚĪ, ḶI ḶĪ, E AI, O AU, AṂ AḤ *

Radiant white, set up counterclockwise, rotate clockwise, 3 or 7 times.

KA KHA GA GHA ṄA
CHA CHHA JA JHA ÑA †
ṬA ṬHA ḌA ḌHA ṆA ‡
TA THA DA DHA NA §
PA PHA BA BHA MA
YA RA LA VA
SHA ṢHA SA HA KṢHAḤ ¶

Red consonants, set up clockwise, rotate counterclockwise, 3 or 7 times.

YE DHARMA-HETU-PRABHAVĀ HETUṂ TEṢHAN TATHAGATO HYAVĀDATTEṢHĀṂ CHA YO NIRODHĀ EVAṂ VĀDĪ MAHĀSHRAMAṆAḤ SVĀHĀ

Yellow letters, set up counterclockwise, rotate clockwise, 3 or 7 times.

(*Tibetan Pronunciation*: *YE DHARMĀ HETU TRABHAVĀ, HETUM TEKHĀM THATĀGATO HYAVADAT, TEKKHĀM TSA YO NIRODHA EWAM WĀDI MAHASHRĀMANA SOHA*)

* In this line, vowels with long diacritical marks are held for two beats; vowels without, for one beat. In the Sanskrit alphabet recitation as a whole, sounds move from the chest (locus of *A*) up the throat (*KA, KHA* ...), to the palate (*CHA, CHHA* ...), to mid-palate (*ṬA, ṬHA, ḌA* ....), to the teeth (*TA, THA Ö*), then lips touching (*PA, PHA Ö*), and lips open (*YA, RA, LA, WA*).
† Tibetans traditionally pronounce these letters *TSA, TSHA, DZA, DZHA, NYA.*
‡ These sounds are retroflex, meaning that the tongue curves back on itself, touching the top of the palate.
§ These sounds are dentals; the tongue touches the back of the top teeth.
¶ Tibetans pronounce these as *SHA KHA ZA HANG KHYAH.*

Calling the Lama

Lama know. Lama know. Lama know.
From faith, an open flower in my heart,
Arise, sole refuge, my kind Lama.
Coarse deeds and failings now afflict me;
Protect me from this difficult lot.
Arise, adorn my great bliss crown's wheel.
Rouse me to be mindful and aware.

FOUR THOUGHTS TO TURN ME FROM SAMSARA

Freedoms, rare life, lost to distraction.
Despite change, death, mind grasps permanence,
Afflictions sway, their effects sure to
Ensnare me in this suffering swirl.
Swift sole refuge, most loving Lama,
Transform these minds, my most kind Lama.
Rare mortal base, take on real meaning;
May I guard pure ethics, leave this swirl.

I. Refuge (*3 times*)

In Three Real Jewels, three root Bliss-Filled Ones;*
Channels, winds, bright orbs—this bodhi-mind;
Essence, nature, moving love mandala,
Until full bodhi,[138] I seek refuge.

II. Bodhicitta Motivation (*3 times*)

HO
Like moons in water, sights deceive us
We ever roam bound in cyclic chains.
So all may rest in their clear mind-sphere,
I raise bodhi through four boundless states.[139]

* Khetsun Sangpo Rinpoche explains that the *sugatas* are the composite of the three roots (guru, deity, and dakini).

III. Vajrasattva (*Dorje Sempa*)

ĀḤ
At my crown, on lotus, moon,
From *HŪṂ*, Lama Dorje Sem.
White, jeweled, clear, with vajra, bell,
Round whose *yab yum*[140] moon-heart *HŪṂ*
Mantra circles, nectar flows,
Cleansing ills, harm,[141] faults, and blocks.

Recite the hundred-syllable mantra:[142]

OṂ BENDZRA SATTVA SAMAYA
MANU PALAYA
BENDZRA SATTVA TVENOPA
TISHTHA DRDHO ME BHAVA
SUTO [KHAYO] ME BHAVA*
SUPO [KHAYO] ME BHAVA
ANU RAKTO ME BHAVA
SARVA SIDDHI ME[143] *TRAYATSHA*
SARVA KARMA SU TSA ME
TSHITAM SHRI YAM KURU HUNG
HA HA HA HA HO
BHAGAVAN SARVA TATHAGATA
BENDZRA MA ME MUN TSA
BENDZRI BHAVA MAHA SAMAYA SATTVA
ĀḤ HŪṂ, PHAṬ[144] (*21 times*)

Dor Sem[145] light melts into me:
Beings: buddhas. Worlds: pure lands.
Recite six syllables: *OṂ BENDZRA SATTVA HŪṂ* (*100 times*)

* In the Adzom lineage, the *TO* of *SUTO* is pronounced very strongly, and *KHAYO* is not pronounced. Similarly, in the next line's *SUPO*, *PO* is pronounced very strongly, and *KHAYO* is not pronounced.

IV. Mandala

OṂ ĀḤ HŪṂ
Three *kāya* lands' oceans in one drop,
Endless such in each tiny atom,
Offered now to refuge ocean so.
Goodness, wisdom, both needs now complete.
IDAṂ GURU RAṬNA MAṆḌALA KAṂ NIR YĀ TA YĀ MI

V. Severance[146]

PHAṬ
Rangrig, great *yum* essence, soars to space
Me-sense, false form, good things for our feast,
Gift-clouds for guests, come enjoy them all.
Be in stainless *dharmakāya* state.
PHAṬ

VI. Guru Yoga

E MA HO
In my-vision Copper Mount,
I am Vajrayogini;
At my crown: lotus, sun, moon.
Lama, one with Lotus Born:
Marks, signs, adornments complete;
Three roots, *rigzin* seas surround—
Clear, great empty-sight sameness.

HŪṂ
Northwest Orgyen's border, there
On a blooming lotus stem:
Powers amazing and supreme,
Widely known as Lotus Born,
With dakinis all around;
I do practice as you did.
Please bring your waves of splendor
Guru, bring me *siddhis*. *HŪṂ*

HRĪḤ
With respect I bow, offer;
Reveal wrongs, rejoice virtue;
Ask you to teach, stay always.
In bright sphere, goodness I share. (*3 times*)

Source of all refuge, Great Guru,
My heart calls, pain unbearable.
Look on me with your compassion;
Please now bestow blessings and *wangs*.[147]

3 times, each recitation followed by one mala of this mantra:
OṂ ĀḤ HŪṂ BENDZRA GURU PEMA SIDDHI HŪṂ

VII. Prayers to the Lineage Lamas

E MA HO
Kunzang, Dorsem, Garab, and Shriseng,
Jampel Shenyen, Jñānasūtra, and
Vima, Lotus Born's king, friend, subject,
Longchen Rabjam, Rigzin Jigme Ling,
Kunzang Shenphen, Gyalwe Nyugu, and
Trime Lodrö, Dorje Ziji Tsel,
Trime Longyong, Gyurme Dorje, and
Pema Wangyal, Pema Trinle Je,
Karma Bendzra, Thupten Gyatso-la[148]—
Pray may our needs both now be fulfilled.

From the letters at lama's three centers, white, red, and blue rays rise in turn, rise at once,
Melt into my three centers in turn, melt at once.
Body, speech, and mind failed pledges cleansed, blessings come,
Four *wangs* gained, four veils[149] gone.
Four *rigzin* seeds are planted;
The four *buddhakāya* states are placed within me.

Mixing [the guru's] heart-mind with my mind, I mentally recite [the mantra]:

OṂ ĀḤ HŪṂ BENDZRA GURU PEMA SIDDHI HŪṂ

Lama melts to light, dissolves in me, great uncontrived spontaneity.
ĀḤ ĀḤ ĀḤ

Close-Lineage Prayer

Awareness-holder Gyurme Dorje,
Pema Wang-gi Gyal, majesty's child,
And Jetsun Kunzang Chime Wangmo:
May my practice come to completion.
—Written by Gyurme Dorje. Virtue.

Sharing the Merit (*Three Dedication Prayers*)

By this good may I swiftly
Once become a great guru,
Lead all beings, every one,
To reach to that very ground.

In all lives, may I good lamas meet,
Never part and rich in Dharma be,
Complete all grounds, paths, good qualities,
Swiftly attain the Dorje Chang[150] state.

Able teacher, treasure jewel Longchen,
Holder of his teaching, Jigme Ling,
Peerless lama's words until world's end,
We hear, think, meditate your teaching.

Colophon

From the expanse of the self-arisen state of Rigzin Jigme Lingpa came forth the great path of luminous, miraculously occurring Dzogchen, this closest of paths, harmonious with all Sutric and Tantric vehicles. I myself, an ordinary person, without any bold intent to elaborate or condense his excellent and profound vajra words, am indeed embarrassed and contrite at heart because of the damage to his blessings.

Yet, in this degenerate time, due to the great force of afflictions and laziness, people find they are not up to virtue and purification, and "Something like this is necessary," said my faithful student, a great teacher at an American school, Anne Klein, whose Dharma name is Rigzin Drolma, and so forth, and who asked me again and again for the sake of many students to do this. So, in the southeastern American city of Houston, Gyurme Thupten Gyatso, called Adzom Tulku, wrote what came to his mind through the base with respect to many excellent texts of the *Heart Essence, the Vast Expanse* foundational practices.

Any faults there may be in this writing are acknowledged before the three roots. May this virtue be a cause for all beings to follow the awareness-bearing (rigzin) lama.

SARVA MANGALAṂ

Further Prayers

These can be linked with any practice session.

LONG-LIFE PRAYER FOR ADZOM GYALSE PAYLO RINPOCHE

OṂ SWASTI
Flawless refuge sources give blessings:
Teacher, protector, kind Dharma lord,
Gyurme Thupten Gyatso, wondrous, good,
Lotus feet ever, deeds everywhere be.

—Prayed by a respectful, virtuous student.

RECITATION AFTER DEDICATION

Things, sounds, minds are gods, mantras, Sheer-forms,
Kayas and wisdom in endless play.
Through this profound and secret practice
Be one with the one taste heart-*thigle*.

COMMENTARY BY ADZOM RINPOCHE WITH VERSE IN ITALICS [NOT RECITED.]

I.

Whatsoever *appearances*, that is, the things or objects appearing to the senses or to the mind, whatsoever *sounds*, whether human or nonhuman, whatsoever *minds*, whether conceptual or ordinary direct perception, these are the three: *deity*, *mantra* (*ngag*), and (the formless) *Sheer-form*, *dharmakāya* (*chöku*).

II.

When you fully realize this view and this practice, everything is the *endless* or infinite *play*ful display of *kayas*, *buddha-bodies* of light, and *primordial wisdom*.

These are the stainless and spontaneous displays of reality (*chö nyi*) itself; like the rays of the sun they are utterly pure, for all impure appearances have vanished.

III.

May the person who completes this deep—that is, *profound* and difficult to understand—practice of this great *Ati* yoga, which is also *secret* such that only the fortunate can understand it

IV.

thereby become *one with* or inseparable from realization. May the self-risen, effortless, indestructible *thigle* be the very center of this practitioner's heart, an inner luminosity that is the youthful vase body. May such practitioners become buddhas for whom there is no bias, for whom all is of *one taste* so that infinite benefit will arise.

These instructions were given to the translator, Rigzin Drolma, orally in July, 2002, at Adzom Gar [Sichuan].

PRAYER TO THE *HEART ESSENCE* (*NYINGTHIG*) PROTECTORS

> *HŪṂ*
> Glorious Ekazati and
> Rishi-Vishnu Rahula,

Oath-bound Dorje Legpa, all
Heart Essence guardian hosts,
Take pledge *tormas* of nectar.
Guard this yogi, give refuge;
Keep your trust, your deeds alive.
I make this virtuous offering in accordance with the
heart request of Lama Shenphen from Ma Gom.

FAITHFUL STUDENT SONG

Advice Exhorting Students to Turn from Samsara, an Excellent Path to Liberation

I ask precious Three Gems,
From deep in my pained heart,
See me with compassion,
I have no other hope.
This dear human body,
Impermanence besets.
Do you not fear your death,
Good and faithful student?

The five *skandhas*[151] gather
And disperse, who knows when.
Heartily think on death,
Good and faithful student.

Karma never deceives
So give up wrongful thoughts.
Engage Dharma holy,
Good and faithful student.

This false swirl will deceive:
Be free of attachment,
Pursue liberation,
Good and faithful student.

Your mind not two pointed,
With unchanging faithful love;
Lama walks with *loma*,*
Good and faithful student.

Gyurme Thupten Gyatso,
When heart holds him lama,
There's no better guidance.
Keep heart talk in your heart.
A HO A LA LA HO!
Pleasing, play-song I offer.
A HO A LA LA HO!
Pleasing, play-song I offer.

* *Loma* is an endearing Tibetan term for "student."

Threefold Epilogue

BY KHETSUN SANGPO RINPOCHE

I.

Please heed what I say here: For anyone wishing to traverse that excellent path known as profound Secret Mantra, there is no way to do so without this. When it comes to teachings on the outer, inner, and secret foundational practices, one must be assiduous and thorough. For one who proceeds in that way, from the beginning and without error, what need is there to mention that the teachings of the actual core and the superbly excellent fruition are as fine and excellent as the causes themselves?

Therefore, so that you may fulfill your hopes and wishes in this way, an old teacher from far away passes along this message to you, this heartfelt advice. Keep it in your heart, and practice the essential spiritual instructions.

II.

In the spacious open realm, in the sky-like purity of basic space itself,
Are infinite hosts of apparitional peaceful and wrathful deities
With boundless compassion for all kinds of disciples,
They take up inconceivable activities in response to whatever they need:
Limitless benefit for all who encounter them.

Beyond childish thoughts and words such as my own—
E MA! This is wondrous!
Once having gathered together

The full heart-meaning from the entire spectrum of teachings,
These most special instructions, the foundational practice teachings, were spoken.

Relying on these,
All your accumulated defilements are purified.
The excellent beings have said:
"This is a fine and flawless path.
There is nothing else like it."

So have confidence.
This fine path has been translated, checked, and ascertained.
(The language is different, but the meaning, the same.)*

III.
Determine the scriptures with awareness and clarity,
Then be steadfast.
These garland-like words, the heart-meaning,
Are offered for your ears so that
You may again and again
See purely how things are.
So be it!

—Khetsun Sangpo Rinpoche

* Rinpoche added this line in his commentary; it does not appear in the Tibetan.

Part Three

Tibetan Texts

Foreword

BY ADZOM RINPOCHE

ཀློང་ཆེན་སྙིང་ཏིག་ཞེས་པ་ནི་རྒྱལ་བ་ཀློང་ཆེན་པའི་དགོངས་བརྒྱུད་ཀྱི་བྱིན་རླབས་འཕོས་པ་ཀུན་མཁྱེན་འཇིགས་མེད་གླིང་པའི་ཐུགས་ཟག་མེད་ཡེ་ཤེས་ཀྱི་ཀློང་ནས་བརྡོལ་བའི་དགོངས་གཏེར་རིམ་དགུའི་ཐེག་པ་ཀུན་དང་མཐུན་ཞིང་ཀུན་ལས་ཁྱད་པར་དུ་མས་འཕགས་པ་མདོ་རྒྱུད་ཀྱི་ལམ་གནད་གཅིག་ཏུ་ཚང་བའི་འོད་གསལ་རྫོགས་པ་ཆེན་པོའི་གཞི་ལམ་འབྲས་གསུམ་གྱི་སྙིང་བཅུད་མ་ལུས་པ་འབྱུང་བའི་ཡང་གསང་བླ་ན་མེད་པའི་ལམ་འདི་ཉིད་བརྒྱུད་ཐག་ཉེ་ཞིང་བྱིན་རླབས་མྱུར་བའི་གདམས་ཁྲིད་ཟབ་མོ་སྔོན་འགྲོ་དང་དངོས་གཞི་གཉིས་ཡོད་པ་ལས་འདིར་ལས་དང་པོ་བ་འཇུག་བདེ་བའི་སྔོན་འགྲོ་ཆེས་ཟབ་རྨད་དུ་བྱུང་བ་རྫོགས་པ་ཆེན་པོའི་ལམ་ལ་འཇུག་པའི་སྒོ་ནས་མིང་སྔོན་འགྲོ་བཏགས་ཀྱང་དོན་ལ་དངོས་གཞི་ཡིན་པས་ཆོས་རྒྱུན་འཛིན་པ་རྣམས་ཀྱི་ཡིད་ཆེས་དད་པས་དང་དུ་བླང་ནས་བློ་སྦྱོང་གནད་སྨིན་དང་བསགས་སྦྱང་ཡང་ཡང་གནང་ནས་ས་ལམ་གྱི་ཡོན་ཏན་ཅིག་ཆར་དུ་བསྐྱོད་པའི་ཐབས་བླ་ན་མེད་པ་ཡིན་པས་ཉམས་ལེན་མཐར་ཕྱིན་པ་མཛད་པར་ཞུ།

དེང་རྫོགས་པ་ཆེན་པོའི་སྔོན་འགྲོ་དང་དངོས་གཞི་ལམ་འདི་ལ་མོས་ཤིང་མཐར་ཕྱིན་པས་རང་སློབ་དམ་པ་མཁས་དབང་ཆེན་མོ་ལོ་རྩ་བ་ཨན་ཁེ་ལན་ནམ་ཆོས་མིང་རིག་འཛིན་སྒྲོལ་མ་མཆོག་ནས་བསྒྱུར་སྒྲིལ་བགྱིས་པ་ལ་ཐུགས་རྗེ་ཆེ་ཞུ།

རེ་གེ་དགོན་ཆེན་ཆོས་སྒར་ནས་ཨ་འཛོམས་སྤྲུལ་མིང་པ་པད་བློ་ནས་ཟླ་བ་༩་པའི་ཚེས་༢༥་ཉིན་ནས།

*Heart Essence, the Vast Expanse**

BY RIGZIN JIGME LINGPA

Calling the Lama

སྔོན་བླ་མ་རྒྱངས་འབོད་ནི།

བླ་མ་མཁྱེན། བླ་མ་མཁྱེན། བླ་མ་མཁྱེན།

ཞེས་ལན་གསུམ་གྱིས་གདུང་བ་དྲག་པོས་བོས་ནས།

སྙིང་དབུས་དད་པའི་གེ་སར་བཞད་པ་ནས།

སྐྱབས་གཅིག་དྲིན་ཅན་བླ་མ་ཡར་ལ་བཞེངས།

ལས་དང་ཉོན་མོངས་དྲག་པོས་གཟིར་བ་ཡི།

སྐལ་པ་ངན་པ་བདག་ལ་སྐྱོབ་པའི་ཕྱིར།

སྤྱི་བོ་བདེ་ཆེན་འཁོར་ལོའི་རྒྱན་དུ་བཞུགས།

དྲན་དང་ཤེས་བཞིན་ཀུན་ཀྱང་བཞེངས་སུ་གསོལ།

* Thanks to Tulku Thondup, Adzom Rinpoche, Tulku Gyurme Tsering, Khetsun Rinpoche, Torchi Lama, Lhoppön Rechung, and Jermay for checking the Tibetan. Tulku Thondup's published Tibetan version in *The Dzogchen Innermost Essence* was used as a reference as was an undated Tibetan edition given to me in 1974.

THE COMMON FOUNDATIONAL PRACTICES

I. Gratitude for My Precious Life

ད་རེས་དམྱལ་བ་ཡི་དྭགས་དུད་འགྲོ་དང་།
ཚེ་རིང་ལྷ་དང་ཀླ་ཀློ་ལོག་ལྟ་ཅན།
སངས་རྒྱས་མ་བྱོན་ཞིང་དང་ལྐུགས་པ་སྟེ།
མི་ཁོམ་བརྒྱད་ལས་ཐར་པའི་དལ་བ་ཐོབ།
མིར་གྱུར་དབང་པོ་ཚང་དང་ཡུལ་དབུས་སྐྱེས།
ལས་མཐའ་མ་ལོག་བསྟན་ལ་དད་པ་སྟེ།
རང་ཉིད་འབྱོར་བ་ལྔ་ཚང་སངས་རྒྱས་བྱོན།
ཆོས་གསུངས་བསྟན་པ་གནས་དང་དེ་ལ་ཞུགས།
བཤེས་གཉེན་དམ་པས་ཟིན་དང་གཞན་འབྱོར་ལྔ།
ཐམས་ཅད་རང་ལ་ཚང་བའི་གནས་ཐོབ་ཀྱང་།
རྐྱེན་མང་ངེས་པ་མེད་པའི་ཆོས་སྤངས་ནས།
འཇིག་རྟེན་ཕ་རོལ་ཉིད་དུ་སོན་པར་འགྱུར།
བློ་སྣ་ཆོས་ལ་བསྒྱུར་ཅིག་གུ་རུ་མཁྱེན།
ལམ་གོལ་དམན་པར་མ་གཏོང་ཀུན་མཁྱེན་རྗེ།
གཉིས་སུ་མེད་དོ་དྲིན་ཅན་བླ་མ་མཁྱེན།

APPRECIATION OF THIS FORTUNATE HUMAN LIFE

ད་རེས་དལ་རྟེན་དོན་ཡོད་མ་བྱས་ན།
ཕྱིས་ནས་ཐར་པ་བསྒྲུབ་པའི་རྟེན་མི་རྙེད།

བདེ་འགྲོའི་རྟེན་ལ་བསོད་ནམས་ཟད་གྱུར་ན།
ཤི་བའི་འོག་ཏུ་ངན་སོང་ངན་འགྲོར་འཁྱམས།
དགེ་སྡིག་མི་ཤེས་ཆོས་ཀྱི་སྒྲ་མི་ཐོས།
དགེ་བའི་བཤེས་དང་མི་མཇལ་མཚང་རེ་ཆེ།

སེམས་ཅན་ཙམ་གྱི་གྲངས་དང་རིམ་པ་ལ།
བསམས་ན་མི་ལུས་ཐོབ་པ་སྲིད་མཐའ་ཙམ།
མི་ཡང་ཆོས་མེད་སྡིག་ལ་སྤྱོད་མཐོང་ན།
ཆོས་བཞིན་སྤྱོད་པ་ཉིན་མོའི་སྐར་མ་ཙམ།
བློ་སྣ་ཆོས་ལ་བསྒྱུར་ཅིག་གུ་རུ་མཁྱེན།
ལམ་གོལ་དམན་པར་མ་གཏོང་ཀུན་མཁྱེན་རྗེ།
གཉིས་སུ་མེད་དོ་དྲིན་ཅན་བླ་མ་མཁྱེན།

THE EIGHT CONTRARY CIRCUMSTANCES

གལ་ཏེ་མི་ལུས་རིན་ཆེན་གླིང་ཕྱིན་ཡང་།
ལུས་རྟེན་བཟང་ལ་བྱུར་པོ་ཆེ་ཡི་སེམས།
ཐར་པ་བསྒྲུབ་པའི་རྟེན་དུ་མི་རུང་ཞིང་།
ཁྱད་པར་བདུད་ཀྱིས་ཟིན་དང་དུག་ལྔ་འཁྲུགས།
ལས་ངན་ཐོག་ཏུ་བབས་དང་ལེ་ལོས་གཡེངས།
གཞན་ཁོལ་བྲན་གཡོག་འཇིགས་སྐྱོབ་ཆོས་ལྟར་བཅོས།
རྨོངས་སོགས་འཕྲལ་བྱུང་རྐྱེན་གྱི་མི་ཁོམ་བརྒྱད།
བདག་ལ་ཆོས་ཀྱི་འགལ་ཟླར་ལྷགས་པའི་ཚེ།
བློ་སྣ་ཆོས་ལ་བསྒྱུར་ཅིག་གུ་རུ་མཁྱེན།
ལམ་གོལ་དམན་པར་མ་གཏོང་ཀུན་མཁྱེན་རྗེ།
གཉིས་སུ་མེད་དོ་དྲིན་ཅན་བླ་མ་མཁྱེན།

THE EIGHT COUNTER-INCLINATIONS

སྐྱོ་ཤས་ཆུང་ཞིང་དད་པའི་ནོར་དང་བྲལ།
འདོད་སྲེད་ཞགས་པས་བཅིངས་དང་ཀུན་སྤྱོད་རྩུབ།
མི་དགེ་སྡིག་ལ་མི་འཛེམ་ལས་མཐའ་ལོག

སྡོམ་པ་ཉམས་ཤིང་དམ་ཚིག་རལ་བ་སྟེ།
རིས་ཆད་བློ་ཡི་མི་ཁོམ་རྣམ་པ་བརྒྱད།
བདག་ལ་ཆོས་ཀྱི་འགལ་ཟླར་ལྷགས་པའི་ཚེ།
བློ་སྣ་ཆོས་ལ་བསྒྱུར་ཅིག་གུ་རུ་མཁྱེན།
ལམ་གོལ་དམན་པར་མ་གཏོང་ཀུན་མཁྱེན་རྗེ།
གཉིས་སུ་མེད་དོ་དྲིན་ཅན་བླ་མ་མཁྱེན།

II. Impermanence

ད་ལྟ་ནད་དང་སྡུག་བསྔལ་གྱིས་མ་གཟིར།
བྲན་འཁོལ་ལ་སོགས་གཞན་དབང་མ་གྱུར་པས།
རང་དབང་ཐོབ་པའི་རྟེན་འབྲེལ་འགྲིག་དུས་འདིར།
སྙོམས་ལས་དང་དུ་དལ་འབྱོར་ཆུད་གསོན་ན།
འཁོར་དང་ལོངས་སྤྱོད་ཉེ་དུ་འབྲེལ་བ་ལྟ།
ལྟ་ཅི་གཅེས་པར་བཟུང་བའི་ལུས་འདི་ཡང་།
མལ་གྱི་ནང་ནས་ས་ཕྱོགས་སྟོང་པར་བསྐྱལ།
ཝ་དད་བྱ་རྒོད་ཁྱི་ཡིས་འདྲུད་པའི་དུས།
བར་དོའི་ཡུལ་ན་འཇིགས་པ་ཤིན་ཏུ་ཆེ།
བློ་སྣ་ཆོས་ལ་བསྒྱུར་ཅིག་གུ་རུ་མཁྱེན།
ལམ་གོལ་དམན་པར་མ་གཏོང་ཀུན་མཁྱེན་རྗེ།
གཉིས་སུ་མེད་དོ་དྲིན་ཅན་བླ་མ་མཁྱེན།

III. Karma: Cause and Effect of Actions

དགེ་སྡིག་ལས་ཀྱི་རྣམ་སྨིན་ཕྱི་བཞིན་འབྲང་།

IV. Sufferings of Samsara

EIGHT HOT HELLS

ཁྱད་པར་དམྱལ་བའི་འཇིག་རྟེན་ཉིད་སོན་ན།
ལྕགས་བསྲེགས་གཞིར་མཚོན་གྱིས་མགོ་ལུས་འདྲལ།
སོག་ལེས་གཤོག་དང་ཐོ་ལུམ་འབར་བས་འཚེར།
སྒོ་མེད་ལྕགས་ཁྱིམ་འཐུམས་པར་ངོ་དོད་འབོད།
འབར་བའི་གསལ་ཤིང་གིས་འབུགས་ཁྲོ་ཆུར་འཚོད།
ཀུན་ནས་ཚ་བའི་མེས་བསྲེགས་བརྒྱད་ཚན་གཅིག

EIGHT COLD HELLS

གངས་རི་སྨུག་པོའི་འདབས་དང་ཆུ་འཁྱགས་ཀྱི།
གཅོང་རོང་ཡ་ངའི་གནས་སུ་བུ་ཡུག་སྤྲིབས།
གྲང་རེག་རླུང་གིས་བཏབ་པའི་ལང་ཚོ་ནི།
ཆུ་བུར་ཅན་དང་ལྷག་པར་བརྡོལ་བ་ཅན།
སྨྲེ་སྔགས་རྒྱུན་མི་ཆད་པར་འདོན་པ་ཡང་།
ཚོར་བའི་སྡུག་བསྔལ་བརྟག་པར་དཀའ་བ་ཡིས།
ཟུངས་ཀྱིས་རབ་བཏང་འཆི་ཁའི་ནད་པ་བཞིན།
ཤུགས་རིང་འདོན་ཅིང་སོ་ཐམ་པགས་པ་འགས།
ཤའུ་ཐོན་ནས་ལྷག་པར་འགས་ཏེ་བརྒྱད།

FOUR NEIGHBORING HELLS

དེ་བཞིན་སྤུ་གྲིའི་ཐང་ལ་རྐང་པ་གཤོགས།
རལ་གྲིའི་ཚལ་དུ་ལུས་ལ་བཅད་གཏུབས་བྱེད།
རོ་མྱགས་འདམ་རྫུད་ཐལ་ཚན་རབ་མེད་ཀློང་།

TWO LESSER HELLS

མནར་བའི་ཉེ་འཁོར་བ་དང་འགྱུར་བ་ཅན།
སྒོ་དང་ཀ་བ་ཐབ་དང་ཐག་པ་སོགས།
རྟག་ཏུ་བཀོལ་ཞིང་སྤྱོད་པའི་ཉི་ཚེ་བ།
རྣམ་གྲངས་བཅོ་བརྒྱད་གང་ལས་འབྱུང་བའི་རྒྱུ།
ཞེ་སྡང་དྲག་པོའི་ཀུན་སློང་སྐྱེས་པའི་ཚེ།
བློ་སྣ་ཆོས་ལ་བསྒྱུར་ཅིག་གུ་རུ་མཁྱེན།
ལམ་གོལ་དམན་པར་མ་གཏོང་ཀུན་མཁྱེན་རྗེ།
གཉིས་སུ་མེད་དོ་དྲིན་ཅན་བླ་མ་མཁྱེན།

HUNGRY GHOSTS

དེ་བཞིན་ཡོངས་ལ་ཉམས་མི་དགའ་བའི་ཡུལ།
བཟའ་བཏུང་ལོངས་སྤྱོད་མིང་ཡང་མི་གྲགས་པར།
ཟས་སྐོམ་ལོ་བླར་མི་རྙེད་ཡི་དྭགས་ལུས།
རིད་ཅིང་ལྡང་བའི་སྟོབས་ཉམས་རྣམ་པ་གསུམ།
གང་ལས་འབྱུང་བའི་རྒྱུ་ནི་སེར་སྣ་ཡིན།

ANIMALS

གཅིག་ལ་གཅིག་ཟ་གསོད་པའི་འཇིགས་པ་ཆེ།
བཀོལ་ཞིང་སྤྱོད་པས་ཉམ་ཐག་བླང་དོར་རྨོངས།
ཕ་མཐའ་མེད་པའི་སྡུག་བསྔལ་གྱིས་གཟིར་བའི།
ས་བོན་གཏི་མུག་མུན་པར་འཁྱམས་པ་བདག
བློ་སྣ་ཆོས་ལ་བསྒྱུར་ཅིག་གུ་རུ་མཁྱེན།
ལམ་གོལ་དམན་པར་མ་གཏོང་ཀུན་མཁྱེན་རྗེ།
གཉིས་སུ་མེད་དོ་དྲིན་ཅན་བླ་མ་མཁྱེན།

V. Recognizing One's Lapses: Relying on a Spiritual Friend

ཆོས་ལམ་ཞུགས་ཀྱང་ཉེས་སྤྱོད་མི་སྡོམ་ཞིང་།

ཐེག་ཆེན་སྒོར་ཞུགས་གཞན་ཕན་སེམས་དང་བྲལ།

དབང་བཞི་ཐོབ་ཀྱང་བསྐྱེད་རྫོགས་མི་སྒོམ་པའི།

ལམ་གོལ་འདི་ལས་བླ་མས་བསྒྲལ་དུ་གསོལ།

ལྟ་བ་མ་རྟོགས་ཐོ་ཅོའི་སྤྱོད་པ་ཅན།

སྒོམ་པ་ཡེངས་ཀྱང་གོ་ཡུལ་ཞུད་གོག་འཐག

སྤྱོད་པ་ནོར་ཀྱང་རང་སྐྱོན་མི་སེམས་པའི།

ཆོས་དྲེད་འདི་ལས་བླ་མས་བསྒྲལ་དུ་གསོལ།

ནངས་པར་འཆི་ཡང་གནས་གོས་ནོར་ལ་སྲེད།

ན་ཚོད་ཡོལ་ཡང་ངེས་འབྱུང་སྐྱོ་ཤས་བྲལ།

ཐོས་པ་ཆུང་ཡང་ཡོན་ཏན་ཅན་དུ་རློམ།

མ་རིག་འདི་ལས་བླ་མས་བསྒྲལ་དུ་གསོལ།

རྐྱེན་ཁར་འཚོར་ཡང་འདུ་འཛི་གནས་སྐོར་སེམས།

དབེན་པར་བརྟེན་ཀྱང་རང་རྒྱུད་ཤིང་ལྟར་རེངས།

དུལ་བར་སྨྲ་ཡང་ཆགས་སྡང་མ་ཞིག་པའི།

ཆོས་བརྒྱད་འདི་ལས་བླ་མས་བསྒྲལ་དུ་གསོལ།

གཉིད་འཐུག་འདི་ལས་མྱུར་དུ་སད་དུ་གསོལ།

ཁྲི་མུན་འདི་ལས་མྱུར་དུ་དབྱུང་དུ་གསོལ།།

THE UNCOMMON FOUNDATIONAL PRACTICES

I. Refuge

དཀོན་མཆོག་གསུམ་དངོས་བདེ་གཤེགས་རྩ་བ་གསུམ༔

རྩ་རླུང་ཐིག་ལེའི་རང་བཞིན་བྱང་ཆུབ་སེམས༔

ངོ་བོ་རང་བཞིན་ཐུགས་རྗེའི་དཀྱིལ་འཁོར་ལ༔

བྱང་ཆུབ་སྙིང་པོའི་བར་དུ་སྐྱབས་སུ་མཆི༔

II. Bodhicitta Motivation

ཧོཿ སྣ་ཚོགས་སྣང་བ་ཆུ་ཟླའི་རྫུན་རིས་ཀྱིཿ
འཁོར་བ་ལུ་གུ་རྒྱུད་དུ་འཁྱམས་པའི་འགྲོཿ
རང་རིག་འོད་གསལ་དབྱིངས་སུ་ངལ་བསོའི་ཕྱིརཿ
ཚད་མེད་བཞི་ཡི་ངང་ནས་སེམས་བསྐྱེད་དོཿ *(3 times)*

III. Vajrasattva

ཨཱཿ བདག་ཉིད་ཐ་མལ་སྤྱི་བོ་རུཿ
པད་དཀར་ཟླ་བའི་གདན་གྱི་དབུསཿ
ཧཱུྃ་ལས་བླ་མ་རྡོ་རྗེ་སེམསཿ
དཀར་གསལ་ལོངས་སྤྱོད་རྫོགས་པའི་སྐུཿ
རྡོ་རྗེ་དྲིལ་འཛིན་སྙེམས་མ་འཁྲིལཿ
ཁྱོད་ལ་སྐྱབས་གསོལ་སྡིག་པ་སྦྱོངཿ
འགྱོད་སེམས་དྲག་པོས་མཐོལ་ལོ་བཤགསཿ
ཕྱིན་ཆད་སྲོག་ལ་བབ་ཀྱང་སྡོམཿ
ཁྱོད་ཐུགས་ཟླ་བ་རྒྱས་པའི་སྟེངཿ
ཧཱུྃ་ཡིག་མཐའ་མར་སྔགས་ཀྱིས་བསྐོརཿ
བཟླས་པ་སྔགས་ཀྱིས་རྒྱུད་བསྐུལ་བསཿ
ཡབ་ཡུམ་བདེ་རོལ་སྦྱོར་མཚམས་ནསཿ
བདུད་རྩི་བྱང་ཆུབ་སེམས་ཀྱི་སྤྲིནཿ
ག་བུར་རྡུལ་ལྟར་འཛག་པ་ཡིསཿ
བདག་དང་ཁམས་གསུམ་སེམས་ཅན་གྱིཿ
ལས་དང་ཉོན་མོངས་སྡུག་བསྔལ་རྒྱུཿ
ནད་གདོན་སྡིག་སྒྲིབ་ཉེས་ལྟུང་གྲིབཿ
མ་ལུས་བྱང་བར་མཛད་དུ་གསོལཿ

THE HUNDRED-SYLLABLE MANTRA:

ཨོཾ་བཛྲ་སཏྭ་ས་མ་ཡ༔ མ་ནུ་པ་ལ་ཡ༔
བཛྲ་སཏྭ་ཏྭེ་ནོ་པ༔ ཏིཥྛ་དྲི་ཌྷོ་མེ་བྷ་ཝ༔
སུ་ཏོ་ཥྱོ་མེ་བྷ་ཝ༔ སུ་པོ་ཥྱོ་མེ་བྷ་ཝ༔
ཨ་ནུ་རཀྟོ་མེ་བྷ་ཝ༔ སརྦ་སིདྡྷི་མྨེ་པྲ་ཡཙྪ༔
སརྦ་ཀརྨ་སུ་ཙ་མེ༔ ཙིཏྟཾ་ཤྲེ་ཡཾ༔ཀུ་རུ་ཧཱུྃ༔
ཧ་ཧ་ཧ་ཧ་ཧོ༔ བྷ་ག་ཝཱན་སརྦ་ཏ་ཐཱ་ག་ཏ༔
བཛྲ་མཱ་མེ་མུཉྩ༔ བཛྲཱི་བྷ་ཝ་མ་ཧཱ་ས་མ་ཡ་སཏྭ་ཨཱཿ

མགོན་པོ་བདག་ནི་མི་ཤེས་རྨོངས་པ་ཡིས༔
དམ་ཚིག་ལས་ནི་འགལ་ཞིང་ཉམས༔
བླ་མ་མགོན་པོས་སྐྱབས་མཛོད་ཅིག༔
གཙོ་བོ་རྡོ་རྗེ་འཛིན་པ་སྟེ༔

ཐུགས་རྗེ་ཆེན་པོའི་བདག་ཉིད་ཅན༔
འགྲོ་བའི་གཙོ་ལ་བདག་སྐྱབས་མཆི༔

Recite respectfully:

སྐུ་གསུང་ཐུགས་རྩ་བ་དང་ཡན་ལག་གི་དམ་ཚིག་ཉམས་པ་
ཐམས་ཅད་མཐོལ་ལོ་བཤགས་སོ༔
སྡིག་པ་དང་སྒྲིབ་པ་ཉེས་ལྟུང་དྲི་མའི་ཚོགས་ཐམས་ཅད་བྱང་
ཞིང་དག་པར་མཛད་དུ་གསོལ༔
ཅེས་བརྗོད་པས་རྡོ་རྗེ་སེམས་དཔའ་དགྱེས་བཞིན་འཛུམ་པ་དང་
བཅས་པས་རིགས་ཀྱི་བུ་ཁྱོད་ཀྱི་སྡིག་སྒྲིབ་ཉེས་ལྟུང་ཐམས་
ཅད་དག་པ་ཡིན་ནོ། ཞེས་གནང་བ་བྱིན་ཞིང་།
འོད་དུ་ཞུ་ནས་རང་ལ་ཐིམ་པའི་རྐྱེན་ལས།

རང་ཉིད་ཀུན་རྫོགས་རྡོ་རྗེ་སེམས་དཔའ་སྣང་སྟོང་མེ་ལོང་

ནང་གི་གཟུགས་བརྙན་ལྟ་བུར་གྱུར་པའི་

ཐུགས་སྲོག་ཧཱུྃ་གི་མཐའ་མར་ཡི་གེར་འབྲུ་བཞི་པོ་གསལ་བ་

ལས་འོད་ཟེར་འཕྲོས་ཁམས་གསུམ་སྣོད་བཅུད་དང་བཅས་པ་

རྡོར་སེམས་རིགས་ལྔའི་རྟེན་དང་བརྟེན་པའི་རང་བཞིན་དུ་

སངས་རྒྱས་པར་བསམས་ལ།

ཨོཾ་བཛྲ་ས་ཏྭ་ཧཱུྃ༔

Recite as many times as possible, then remain in equipoise.

IV. Mandala

ཨོཾ་ཨཱཿཧཱུྃ༔

སྟོང་གསུམ་འཇིག་རྟེན་བྱེ་བ་ཕྲག་བརྒྱའི་ཞིང༔

རིན་ཆེན་སྣ་བདུན་ལྷ་མིའི་འབྱོར་པས་གཏམས༔

བདག་ལུས་ལོངས་སྤྱོད་བཅས་པ་ཡོངས་འབུལ་གྱིས༔

ཆོས་ཀྱི་འཁོར་ལོས་སྒྱུར་བའི་སྲིད་ཐོབ་ཤོག༔

འོག་མིན་བདེ་ཆེན་སྟུག་པོ་བཀོད་པའི་ཞིང༔

ངེས་པ་ལྔ་ལྡན་རིགས་ལྔའི་ཚོམ་བུ་ཅན༔

འདོད་ཡོན་མཆོད་པའི་སྤྲིན་ཕུང་བསམས་ཡས་པ༔

ཕུལ་བས་ལོངས་སྐུའི་ཞིང་ལ་སྤྱོད་པར་ཤོག༔

སྣང་སྲིད་རྣམ་དག་གཞོན་ནུ་བུམ་པའི་སྐུ༔

ཐུགས་རྗེ་མ་འགགས་ཆོས་ཉིད་རོལ་པས་བརྒྱན༔

སྐུ་དང་ཐིག་ལེའི་འཛིན་པ་རྣམ་དག་ཞིང༔

ཕུལ་བས་ཆོས་སྐུའི་ཞིང་ལ་སྤྱོད་པར་ཤོག༔

V. Severance: *A Beggar's Way of Accumulating Merit*

ཕཊ༔ ལུས་གཅེས་འཛིན་བོར་བས་ལྷ་བདུད་ཆོམ༔
སེམས་ཚངས་པའི་སྒོ་ནས་དབྱིངས་ལ་ཕོན༔
འཆི་བདག་གི་བདུད་བཅོམ་ཁྲོས་མར་གྱུར༔
གཡས་ཉོན་མོངས་བདུད་བཅོམ་གྱི་གྲི་གུག་གིས༔
གཟུགས་ཕུང་པོའི་བདུད་བཅོམ་ཐོད་པ་བྲེགས༔
གཡོན་ལས་བྱེད་ཚུལ་གྱིས་ཌྷཀྐ་ཐོགས༔
སྐུ་གསུམ་གྱི་མི་མགོའི་སྒྱེད་བུར་བཞག༔
ནང་སྟོང་གསུམ་གང་བའི་བམ་རོ་དེ༔
ཨཱ༔ ཐུང་དང་ཧཾ་ཡིག་གིས་བདུད་རྩིར་བཞུ༔
འབྲུ་གསུམ་གྱི་ནུས་པས་སྦྱང་སྤེལ་བསྒྱུར༔

ཨོཾ་ཨཱ་ཧཱུཾ༔ ཅི་ནུས་བཟླས་མཐར༔
ཕཊ༔ ཡར་མཆོད་ཡུལ་མགྲོན་གྱི་ཐུགས་དམ་བསྐང༔
ཚོགས་རྫོགས་ནས་མཆོག་ཐུན་དངོས་གྲུབ་ཐོབ༔
མར་འཁོར་བའི་མགྲོན་མཉེས་ལན་ཆགས་བྱང༔
ཁྱད་པར་དུ་གནོད་བྱེད་བགེགས་རིགས་ཚིམ༔
ནད་གདོན་དང་བར་ཆད་དབྱིངས་སུ་ཞི༔
རྐྱེན་ངན་དང་བདག་འཛིན་རྡུལ་དུ་བརླགས༔
མཐར་མཆོད་བྱ་དང་མཆོད་བྱེད་མཆོད་ཡུལ་ཀུན༔
གཤིས་རྫོགས་པ་ཆེན་པོར་མ་བཅོས་ཨཱ༔

VI. Guru Yoga

ཨེ་མ་ཧོ༔ རང་སྣང་ལྷུན་གྲུབ་དག་པ་རབ་འབྱམས་ཞིང༔
བཀོད་པ་རབ་རྫོགས་ཟངས་མདོག་དཔལ་རིའི་དབུས༔
རང་ཉིད་རྗེ་བཙུན་* རྡོ་རྗེ་རྣལ་འབྱོར་མ༔
ཞལ་གཅིག་ཕྱག་གཉིས་དམར་གསལ་གྲི་ཐོད་འཛིན༔
ཞབས་གཉིས་དོར་སྟབས་སྤྱན་གསུམ་ནམ་མཁར་གཟིགས༔
སྤྱི་བོར་པདྨ་འབུམ་བརྡལ་ཉི་ཟླའི་སྟེང༔
སྐྱབས་གནས་ཀུན་འདུས་རྩ་བའི་བླ་མ་དང༔
དབྱེར་མེད་མཚོ་སྐྱེས་རྡོ་རྗེ་སྤྲུལ་པའི་སྐུ༔
དཀར་དམར་མདངས་ལྡན་གཞོན་ནུའི་ཤ་ཚུགས་ཅན༔
ཕོད་ཁ་ཆོས་གོས་ཟ་བེར་འདུང་མ་གསོལ༔
ཞལ་གཅིག་ཕྱག་གཉིས་རྒྱལ་པོ་རོལ་པའི་སྟབས༔
ཕྱག་གཡས་རྡོ་རྗེ་གཡོན་པས་ཐོད་བུམ་བསྣམས༔
དབུ་ལ་འདབ་ལྡན་པདྨའི་མཉེན་ཞུ་གསོལ༔
མཆན་ཁུང་གཡོན་ན་བདེ་སྟོང་ཡུམ་མཆོག་མ༔
སྦས་པའི་ཚུལ་གྱིས་ཁ་ཊཾ་རྩེ་གསུམ་བསྣམས༔
འཇའ་ཟེར་ཐིག་ལེའི་འོད་ཕུང་ཀློང་ན་བཞུགས༔
ཕྱི་འཁོར་འོད་ལྔའི་དྲྭ་བས་མཛེས་པའི་ཀློང༔
སྤྲུལ་པའི་རྗེ་འབངས་ཉི་ཤུ་རྩ་ལྔ་དང༔
རྒྱ་བོད་པཎ་གྲུབ་རིག་འཛིན་ཡི་དམ་ལྷ༔
མཁའ་འགྲོ་ཆོས་སྐྱོང་དམ་ཅན་སྤྲིན་ལྟར་གཏིབས༔
གསལ་སྟོང་མཉམ་གནས་ཆེན་པོའི་ངང་དུ་གསལ༔

* Original text referenced read: *rang nyid gzhi lus rdo rje*; it has been changed to read: *rang nyid rje btsun rdo rje* by Adzom Rinpoche.

THE SEVEN-LINE PRAYER

ཧཱུྃ༔ ཨོ་རྒྱན་ཡུལ་གྱི་ནུབ་བྱང་མཚམས༔
པདྨ་གེ་སར་སྡོང་པོ་ལ༔
ཡ་མཚན་མཆོག་གི་དངོས་གྲུབ་བརྙེས༔
པདྨ་འབྱུང་གནས་ཞེས་སུ་གྲགས༔
འཁོར་དུ་མཁའ་འགྲོ་མང་པོས་བསྐོར༔
ཁྱེད་ཀྱི་རྗེས་སུ་བདག་བསྒྲུབ་ཀྱིས༔
བྱིན་གྱིས་བརླབ་ཕྱིར་གཤེགས་སུ་གསོལ༔
གུ་རུ་པདྨ་སིདྡྷི་ཧཱུྃ༔

THE SEVEN-BRANCH PUJA

ཧྲཱི༔ བདག་ལུས་ཞིང་གི་རྡུལ་སྙེད་དུ༔
རྣམ་པར་འཕྲུལ་པས་ཕྱག་འཚལ་ལོ༔
དངོས་བཤམས་ཡིད་སྤྲུལ་ཏིང་འཛིན་མཐུས༔
སྣང་སྲིད་མཆོད་པའི་ཕྱག་རྒྱར་འབུལ༔
སྒོ་གསུམ་མི་དགེའི་ལས་རྣམས་ཀུན༔
འོད་གསལ་ཆོས་སྐུའི་ངང་དུ་བཤགས༔
བདེན་པ་གཉིས་ཀྱིས་བསྡུས་པ་ཡི༔
དགེ་ཚོགས་ཀུན་ལ་རྗེས་ཡི་རང༔
རིགས་ཅན་གསུམ་གྱི་གདུལ་བྱ་ལ༔*
ཐེག་གསུམ་ཆོས་འཁོར་བསྐོར་བར་བསྐུལ༔
ཇི་སྲིད་འཁོར་བ་མ་སྟོངས་བར༔
མྱ་ངན་མི་འདའ་བཞུགས་གསོལ་འདེབས༔
དུས་གསུམ་བསགས་པའི་དགེ་རྩ་ཀུན༔
བྱང་ཆུབ་ཆེན་པོའི་རྒྱུ་རུ་བསྔོ༔

* Inserted by Adzom Rinpoche.

With strong devotion:

ཛེ་བཙུན་གུ་རུ་རིན་པོ་ཆེ༔
ཁྱེད་ནི་སངས་རྒྱས་ཐམས་ཅད་ཀྱི༔
ཐུགས་རྗེ་བྱིན་རླབས་འདུས་པའི་དཔལ༔
སེམས་ཅན་ཡོངས་ཀྱི་མགོན་གཅིག་པུ༔
ལུས་དང་ལོངས་སྤྱོད་བློ་སྙིང་བྲང༔
ལྷོས་པ་མེད་པར་ཁྱེད་ལ་འབུལ༔
འདི་ནས་བྱང་ཆུབ་མ་ཐོབ་བར༔
སྐྱིད་སྡུག་ལེགས་ཉེས་མཐོ་དམན་ཀུན༔
རྗེ་བཙུན་ཆེན་པོ་པད་འབྱུང་མཁྱེན༔

ཨོཾ་ཨཱཿཧཱུྃ་བཛྲ་གུ་རུ་པདྨ་སིདྡྷི་ཧཱུྃ༔ *[100 times]*

With strong feeling, stirring mind and body, recite:

བདག་ལ་རེ་ས་གཞན་ན་མེད༔
ད་ལྟའི་དུས་ངན་སྙིགས་མའི་འགྲོ༔
མི་བཟོད་སྡུག་བསྔལ་འདམ་དུ་བྱིངས༔
འདི་ལས་སྐྱོབས་ཤིག་མ་ཧཱ་གུ་རུ༔
དབང་བཞི་བསྐུར་ཅིག་བྱིན་རླབས་ཅན༔
རྟོགས་པ་སྐྱོར་ཅིག་ཐུགས་རྗེ་ཅན༔
སྒྲིབ་གཉིས་སྦྱོངས་ཤིག་ནུས་མཐུ་ཅན༔

If possible recite one hundred times, or repeat this verse three times, reciting one hundred mantras each time:

ཨོཾ་ཨཱ་ཧཱུྃ་བཛྲ་གུ་རུ་པདྨ་སིདྡྷི་ཧཱུྃ༔

ནམ་ཞིག་ཚེ་ཡི་དུས་བྱས་ཚེ༔
རང་སྣང་རྔ་ཡབ་དཔལ་རིའི་ཞིང༔
ཟུང་འཇུག་སྤྲུལ་པའི་ཞིང་ཁམས་སུ༔
གཞི་ལུས་རྡོ་རྗེ་རྣལ་འབྱོར་མ༔
གསལ་འཚེར་འོད་ཀྱི་གོང་བུ་རུ༔
གྱུར་ནས་རྗེ་བཙུན་པད་འབྱུང་དང༔
དབྱེར་མེད་ཆེན་པོར་སངས་རྒྱས་ཏེ༔
བདེ་དང་སྟོང་པའི་ཆོ་འཕྲུལ་གྱི༔
ཡེ་ཤེས་ཆེན་པོའི་རོལ་པ་ལས༔
ཁམས་གསུམ་སེམས་ཅན་མ་ལུས་པ༔
འདྲེན་པའི་དེད་དཔོན་དམ་པ་རུ༔
རྗེ་བཙུན་པདྨས་དབུགས་དབྱུང་གསོལ༔
གསོལ་བ་སྙིང་གི་དཀྱིལ་ནས་འདེབས༔
ཁ་ཙམ་ཚིག་ཙམ་མ་ཡིན་ནོ༔
བྱིན་རླབས་ཐུགས་ཀྱི་ཀློང་ནས་སྩོལ༔
བསམ་དོན་འགྲུབ་པར་མཛད་དུ་གསོལ༔

ཨོཾ་ཨཱ་ཧཱུྃ་བཛྲ་གུ་རུ་པདྨ་སིདྡྷི་ཧཱུྃ༔ *Repeat many times*

VII. Prayers to the Lineage Lamas

ཨེ་མ་ཧོ༔ རྒྱ་ཆད་ཕྱོགས་ལྷུང་བྲལ་བའི་ཞིང་ཁམས་ནས༔
དང་པོའི་སངས་རྒྱས་ཆོས་སྐུ་ཀུན་ཏུ་བཟང༔
ལོངས་སྐུ་ཆུ་ཟླའི་རོལ་རྩལ་རྡོ་རྗེ་སེམས༔
སྤྲུལ་སྐུར་མཚན་རྫོགས་དགའ་རབ་རྡོ་རྗེ་ལ༔
གསོལ་བ་འདེབས་སོ་བྱིན་རླབས་དབང་བསྐུར་སྩོལ༔

ཤྲཱི་སིངྷ་དོན་དམ་ཆོས་ཀྱི་མཛོད༔
འཇམ་དཔལ་བཤེས་གཉེན་ཐེག་དགུའི་འཁོར་ལོས་སྒྱུར༔
ཛྙཱ་ན་སུ་ཏྲ་པཎ་ཆེན་བི་མ་ལར༔
གསོལ་བ་འདེབས་སོ་གྲོལ་བྱེད་ལམ་སྣ་སྟོན༔

འཛམ་བུ་གླིང་གི་རྒྱན་གཅིག་པདྨ་འབྱུང༔
ངེས་པར་ཐུགས་ཀྱི་སྲས་མཆོག་རྗེ་འབངས་གྲོགས༔
ཐུགས་གཏེར་རྒྱ་མཚོའི་བདག་གྲོལ་ཀློང་ཆེན་ཞབས༔
མཁའ་འགྲོའི་དབྱིངས་མཛོད་བཀའ་བབས་འཇིགས་མེད་གླིང༔
གསོལ་བ་འདེབས་སོ་འབྲས་བུ་ཐོབ་གྲོལ་སྩོལ༔

མཁས་ཤིང་གྲུབ་བརྙེས་ཀུན་བཟང་གཞན་ཕན་དཔལ།
ཕྲུག་ན་པདྨོ་རྒྱལ་བའི་མྱུ་གུ་དང་།
འཇམ་པའི་དབྱངས་དངོས་མཁན་ཆེན་པདྨའི་མཚན།
གསོལ་བ་འདེབས་སོ་གནས་ལུགས་རང་ཞལ་སྟོན།
ཁྱད་པར་ཟབ་མོ་འོད་གསལ་སྙིང་ཐིག་གི
ཤིང་རྟ་ཆེན་པོ་མདོ་སྔགས་གླིང་པའི་ཞབས།
བཀའ་དྲིན་མཉམ་མེད་རྩ་བའི་བླ་མ་ལ།
གསོལ་བ་འདེབས་སོ་དོན་གཉིས་ལྷུན་གྲུབ་མཛོད།

གསང་བདག་དཔའ་བོ་ཀུན་བཟང་གཞན་ཕན་དཔལ༔*

སྤྱན་རས་གཟིགས་དངོས་རྒྱལ་བའི་མྱུ་གུ་དང༔

ཆོས་ཀྱི་སྤྱན་མངའ་དྲི་མེད་བློ་གྲོས་ཞབས༔

བཀའ་ བབས་ བདུན་ ལྡན་ རྡོ་ རྗེ་ གཟི་ བརྗིད་ རྩལ༔

བཀའ་དྲིན་མཉམ་མེད་རྩ་བའི་བླ་མ་ལ༔†

གསོལ་བ་འདེབས་སོ་སྣང་བཞི་མཐར་ཕྱིན་ཤོག༔

Added by Khetsun Sangpo Rinpoche:

མཁས་ཞིང་གྲུབ་བརྙེས་ཀུན་བཟང་གཞན་ཕན་དཔལ་

ཕྱག་ན་པདྨ་རྒྱལ་བའི་མྱུ་གུ་དང་

འཇམ་པའི་དབྱངས་དངོས་མཁན་ཆེན་པདྨའི་མཚན་

གསོལ་བ་འདེབས་སོ་གནས་ལུགས་རང་ཞལ་སྟོན།

Added by Adzom Rinpoche:

རིག་འཛིན་འགྲོ་འདུལ་དཔའ་བོ་རྡོ་རྗེ་དང་

འགྱུར་མེད་རྡོ་རྗེ་པདྨ་དབང་གི་རྒྱལ་

ལྷ་བཙུན་ཀུན་བཟང་འཆི་མེད་དབང་མོ་བཅས་

ཐུབ་བསྟན་པདྨ་ཕྲིན་ལས་དཔལ་བཟང་པོ་

མཁན་ཆེན་དམ་པ་ཀརྨ་བརྫེ་དང་

གསོལ་བ་འདེབས་སོ་དོན་གཉིས་ལྷུན་འགྲུབ་ཤོག

རིག་འཛིན་འགྱུར་མེད་ཐུབ་བསྟན་རྒྱ་མཚོ་ལ་

གསོལ་བ་འདེབས་སོ་ཉམས་ལེན་མཐར་ཕྱིན་ཤོག

* This and the following three lines do not appear in all editions of the text; quite naturally, different monastic groups or branches of transmission will specifically acknowledge their own specific teachers.

† This line is not in Adzom Rinpoche's rendition.

PRAYERFUL ASPIRATIONS FOR THIS LIFE

སྲིད་ལས་ངེས་པར་འབྱུང་བའི་ཞེན་ལོག་གིས༔
རྡོ་རྗེའི་བླ་མ་དོན་ལྡན་མིག་བཞིན་བསྟེན༔
ཅི་གསུང་བཀའ་བསྒྲུབ་ཟབ་མོའི་ཉམས་ལེན་ལ༔
ལྷེམ་ཀྲུང་མེད་པའི་སྒྲུབ་ཚུགས་ཞེ་རུས་ཀྱིས༔
ཐུགས་རྒྱུད་དགོངས་པའི་བྱིན་རླབས་འཕོ་བར་ཤོག༔
སྣང་སྲིད་འཁོར་འདས་ཡེ་ནས་འོག་མིན་ཞིང༔
ལྷ་སྔགས་ཆོས་སྐུར་དག་རྫོགས་སྨིན་པའི་འབྲས༔
སྤང་བླང་བྱ་རྩོལ་མེད་པའི་རྫོགས་པ་ཆེ༔
ཤེས་ཉམས་ཡིད་དཔྱོད་ལས་འདས་རིག་པའི་གདངས༔
ཆོས་ཉིད་མངོན་སུམ་རྗེན་པར་མཐོང་བར་ཤོག༔
མཚན་མའི་རྟོག་པ་རྣམ་གྲོལ་འཇའ་ཟེར་སྦུབས༔
སྐུ་དང་ཐིག་ལེའི་ཉམས་སྣང་གོང་དུ་འཕེལ༔
རིག་རྩལ་ལོངས་སྐུའི་ཞིང་ཁམས་ཚད་ལ་ཕེབས༔
ཆོས་ཟད་བློ་འདས་ཆེན་པོར་སངས་རྒྱས་ཏེ༔
གཞོན་ནུ་བུམ་སྐུར་གཏན་སྲིད་ཟིན་པར་ཤོག༔

PRAYERFUL ASPIRATIONS FOR THE BARDO

ཤིན་ཏུ་རྣལ་འབྱོར་ཉམས་འོག་མ་ཆུད་དེ༔
རགས་ལུས་དྭངས་མའི་དབྱིངས་སུ་མ་གྲོལ་ན༔
ནམ་ཞིག་ཚེ་ཡི་འདུ་བྱེད་བསྡུང་བའི་ཚེ༔
འཆི་བ་འོད་གསལ་ཀ་དག་ཆོས་སྐུར་ཤར༔
བར་དོའི་སྣང་ཆ་ལོངས་སྤྱོད་རྫོགས་སྐུར་གྲོལ༔
ཁྲེགས་ཆོད་ཐོད་རྒལ་ལམ་གྱི་རྩལ་རྫོགས་ནས༔
མ་པང་བུ་འཇུག་ལྟ་བུར་གྲོལ་བར་ཤོག༔

PRAYERFUL ASPIRATIONS FOR THE NEXT LIFE

གསང་ཆེན་འོད་གསལ་ཐེག་པ་མཆོག་གི་རྩེ༔
སངས་རྒྱས་གཞན་ནས་མི་འཚོལ་ཆོས་སྐུའི་ཞལ༔
མངོན་གྱུར་གདོད་མའི་ས་ལ་མ་གྲོལ་ན༔
མ་སྒོམ་སངས་རྒྱས་ཆོས་ལྔའི་ལམ་མཆོག་ལ༔
བརྟེན་ནས་རང་བཞིན་སྤྲུལ་པའི་ཞིང་ལྔ་དང༔
ཁྱད་པར་པདྨ་འོད་ཀྱི་ཕོ་བྲང་དུ༔
རིག་འཛིན་རྒྱ་མཚོའི་གཙོ་མཆོག་ཨོ་རྒྱན་རྗེས༔
གསང་ཆེན་ཆོས་ཀྱི་དགའ་སྟོན་འགྱེད་པའི་སར༔
སྲས་ཀྱི་ཐུ་བོར་སྐྱེས་ནས་དབུགས་དབྱུང་སྟེ༔
མཐའ་ཡས་འགྲོ་བའི་ཉེར་འཚོར་བདག་འགྱུར་ཤོག༔

PRAYER FOR ACHIEVING THESE ASPIRATIONS

རིག་འཛིན་རྒྱལ་བ་རྒྱ་མཚོའི་བྱིན་རླབས་དང༔
ཆོས་དབྱིངས་བསམ་མི་ཁྱབ་པའི་བདེན་པ་ཡིས༔
དཔལ་འབྱོར་རྟེན་ལ་རྫོགས་སྨིན་སྦྱངས་གསུམ་གྱི༔
རྟེན་འབྲེལ་མངོན་གྱུར་སངས་རྒྱས་ཐོབ་པར་ཤོག༔

VIII. Initiation

གུ་རུའི་སྨིན་མཚམས་ནས་ཨོཾ་ཡིག་ཆུ་ཤེལ་ལྟ་བུར་འཚེར་བ་ལས་འོད་ཟེར་འཕྲོས༔
རང་གི་སྤྱི་བོ་ནས་ཞུགས༔
ལུས་ཀྱི་ལས་དང་རྩ་ཡི་སྒྲིབ་པ་དག༔
སྐུ་རྡོ་རྗེའི་བྱིན་རླབས་ཞུགས༔ བུམ་པའི་དབང་ཐོབ༔
བསྐྱེད་རིམ་གྱི་སྣོད་དུ་གྱུར༔
རྣམ་སྨིན་རིག་འཛིན་གྱི་ས་བོན་ཐེབས༔
སྤྲུལ་སྐུའི་གོ་འཕང་ཐོབ་པའི་སྐལ་བ་རྒྱུད་ལ་བཞག༔

མགྲིན་པ་ནས་ཨཱ༔ ཡིག་པདྨ་རཱ་ག་ལྟར་འབར་བ་ལས་འོད་ཟེར་འཕྲོས༔
རང་གི་མགྲིན་པ་ནས་ཞུགས༔
ངག་གི་ལས་དང་རླུང་གི་སྒྲིབ་པ་དག༔
གསུང་རྡོ་རྗེའི་བྱིན་རླབས་ཞུགས༔
གསང་བའི་དབང་ཐོབ༔
བཟླས་བརྗོད་ཀྱི་སྣོད་དུ་གྱུར༔
ཚེ་དབང་རིག་འཛིན་གྱི་ས་བོན་ཐེབས༔
ལོངས་སྤྱོད་རྫོགས་པའི་གོ་འཕང་གི་སྐལ་བ་རྒྱུད་ལ་བཞག༔

ཐུགས་ཀའི་ཧཱུྃ་ཡིག་ནམ་མཁའི་མདོག་ཅན་ལས་འོད་ཟེར་འཕྲོས༔
རང་གི་སྙིང་ག་ནས་ཞུགས༔
ཡིད་ཀྱི་ལས་དང་ཐིག་ལེའི་སྒྲིབ་པ་དག༔
ཐུགས་རྡོ་རྗེའི་བྱིན་རླབས་ཞུགས༔
ཤེས་རབ་ཡེ་ཤེས་ཀྱི་དབང་ཐོབ༔
བདེ་སྟོང་ཙཎྜ་ལིའི་སྣོད་དུ་གྱུར༔
ཕྱག་རྒྱའི་རིག་འཛིན་གྱི་ས་བོན་ཐེབས༔
ཆོས་སྐུའི་གོ་འཕང་ཐོབ་པའི་སྐལ་བ་རྒྱུད་ལ་བཞག༔

སླར་ཡང་ཐུགས་ཀའི་ཧཱུྃ་ལས་ཧཱུྃ་ཡིག་གཉིས་པ་ཞིག་སྐར་མདའ་འཕངས་པ་བཞིན་དུ་ཆད༔
རང་སེམས་དང་ཐ་དད་མེད་པར་འདྲེས༔
ཀུན་གཞིའི་ལས་དང་ཤེས་བྱའི་སྒྲིབ་པ་སྦྱངས༔
ཡེ་ཤེས་རྡོ་རྗེའི་བྱིན་རླབས་ཞུགས༔
ཚིག་གིས་མཚོན་པ་དོན་དམ་གྱི་དབང་ཐོབ༔
ཀ་དག་རྫོགས་པ་ཆེན་པོའི་སྣོད་དུ་གྱུར༔
ལྷུན་གྲུབ་རིག་འཛིན་གྱི་ས་བོན་ཐེབས༔
མཐར་ཐུག་གི་འབྲས་བུ་ངོ་བོ་ཉིད་སྐུའི་སྐལ་པ་རྒྱུད་ལ་བཞག་གོ༔

Silently recite the vajra guru mantra with a sense that you are actually receiving the four initiations.

ནམ་ཞིག་ཚེ་ཡི་དུས་བྱས་ཚེ༔
རང་སྣང་རྔ་ཡབ་དཔལ་རིའི་ཞིང༔
ཟུང་འཇུག་སྤྲུལ་པའི་ཞིང་ཁམས་སུ༔
གཞི་ལུས་རྡོ་རྗེ་རྣལ་འབྱོར་མ༔
གསལ་འཚེར་འོད་ཀྱི་གོང་བུ་རུ༔
གྱུར་ནས་རྗེ་བཙུན་པད་འབྱུང་དང༔
དབྱེར་མེད་ཆེན་པོར་སངས་རྒྱས་ཏེ༔
བདེ་དང་སྟོང་པའི་ཆོ་འཕྲུལ་གྱིས༔
ཡེ་ཤེས་ཆེན་པོའི་རོལ་པ་ལས༔
ཁམས་གསུམ་སེམས་ཅན་མ་ལུས་པ༔
འདྲེན་པའི་དེད་དཔོན་དམ་པ་རུ༔
རྗེ་བཙུན་པདྨས་དབུགས་དབྱུང་གསོལ༔
གསོལ་བ་སྙིང་གི་དཀྱིལ་ནས་འདེབས༔
ཁ་ཙམ་ཚིག་ཙམ་མ་ཡིན་ནོ༔
བྱིན་རླབས་ཐུགས་ཀྱི་ཀློང་ནས་སྩོལ༔
བསམ་དོན་འགྲུབ་པར་མཛད་དུ་གསོལ༔

བླ་མའི་ཐུགས་ཀ་ནས་འོད་ཟེར་དམར་པོ་ཧྲིད་དང་བཅས་པ་ཞིག་ཤལ་གྱིས་བྱུང་བ་བདག་ཉིད་རྡོ་རྗེ་རྣལ་འབྱོར་མར་གསལ་བའི་སྙིང་ཁར་རེག་པ་ཙམ་གྱིས་འོད་དམར་གྱི་གོང་བུ་ཞིག་ཏུ་གྱུར་ནས་གུ་རུ་རིན་པོ་ཆེའི་ཐུགས་ཀར་ཐིམ་པས་དབྱེར་མེད་རོ་གཅིག་ཏུ་གྱུར་པར་བསྒོམ།*

* On page 171 Adzom Rinpoche's version substitutes the phrase *thugs kar thim pas dbyed med ro gcig tu gyur par bsgom* with *thugs kyi thugler ro gcig shog.*

དཔལ་ལྡན་རྩ་བའི་བླ་མ་རིན་པོ་ཆེ།
བདག་གི་སྙིང་གར་པདྨའི་གདན་བཞུགས་ལ།
བཀའ་དྲིན་ཆེན་པོའི་སྒོ་ནས་རྗེས་བཟུང་སྟེ།
སྐུ་གསུང་ཐུགས་ཀྱི་དངོས་གྲུབ་སྩལ་དུ་གསོལ།

དཔལ་ལྡན་བླ་མའི་རྣམ་པར་ཐར་པ་ལ།
སྐད་ཅིག་ཙམ་ཡང་ལོག་ལྟ་མི་སྐྱེ་ཞིང་།
ཅི་མཛད་ལེགས་པར་མཐོང་བའི་མོས་གུས་ཀྱིས།
བླ་མའི་བྱིན་རླབས་སེམས་ལ་འཇུག་པར་ཤོག
སྐྱེ་བ་ཀུན་ཏུ་ཡང་དག་བླ་མ་དང་།
འབྲལ་མེད་ཆོས་ཀྱི་དཔལ་ལ་ལོངས་སྤྱོད་ནས།
ས་དང་ལམ་གྱི་ཡོན་ཏན་རབ་རྫོགས་ཏེ།
རྡོ་རྗེ་འཆང་གི་གོ་འཕང་མྱུར་ཐོབ་ཤོག

Dedication Prayers: Sharing the Goodness of Our Practice

1.

དགེ་བ་འདི་ཡིས་སྐྱེ་བོ་ཀུན།
བསོད་ནམས་ཡེ་ཤེས་ཚོགས་རྫོགས་ཤིང་།
བསོད་ནམས་ཡེ་ཤེས་ལས་བྱུང་བ།
དམ་པ་སྐུ་གཉིས་ཐོབ་པར་ཤོག
འགྲོ་ཀུན་དགེ་བ་ཇི་སྙེད་ཡོད་པ་དང་།
བྱས་དང་བྱེད་འགྱུར་དེ་བཞིན་བྱེད་པ་གང་།
བཟང་པོ་ཇི་བཞིན་དེ་འདྲའི་ས་དག་ལ།
ཀུན་ཀྱང་ཀུན་ནས་བཟང་པོར་རེག་གྱུར་ཅིག

II.

འཇམ་དཔལ་དཔའ་བོས་ཇི་ལྟར་མཁྱེན་པ་དང་།
ཀུན་ཏུ་བཟང་པོ་དེ་ཡང་དེ་བཞིན་ཏེ།
དེ་དག་ཀུན་གྱི་རྗེས་སུ་བདག་སློབ་ཅིང་།
དགེ་བ་འདི་དག་ཐམས་ཅད་རབ་ཏུ་བསྔོ།

III.

དུས་གསུམ་གཤེགས་པའི་རྒྱལ་བ་ཐམས་ཅད་ཀྱིས།
བསྔོ་བ་གང་ལ་མཆོག་ཏུ་བསྔགས་པ་སྟེ།
བདག་གི་དགེ་བའི་རྩ་བ་འདི་ཀུན་ཀྱང་།
བཟང་པོ་སྤྱོད་ཕྱིར་རབ་ཏུ་བསྔོ་བར་བགྱི།

SPECIAL ASPIRATION

གང་དུ་སྐྱེས་པའི་སྐྱེ་བ་ཐམས་ཅད་དུ།
མཐོ་རིས་ཡོན་ཏན་བདུན་ལྡན་ཐོབ་པར་ཤོག
སྐྱེས་མ་ཐག་ཏུ་ཆོས་དང་འཕྲད་གྱུར་ཅིང་།
ཚུལ་བཞིན་བསྒྲུབ་པའི་རང་དབང་ཡོད་པར་ཤོག
དེར་ཡང་བླ་མ་དམ་པ་མཉེས་བྱེད་ཅིང་།
ཉིན་དང་མཚན་དུ་ཆོས་ལ་སྤྱོད་པར་ཤོག
ཆོས་རྟོགས་ནས་ནི་སྙིང་པོའི་དོན་བསྒྲུབས་ཏེ།
ཚེ་དེས་སྲིད་པའི་རྒྱ་མཚོ་བརྒལ་བར་ཤོག
སྲིད་པར་དམ་པའི་ཆོས་རབ་སྟོན་བྱེད་ཅིང་།
གཞན་ཕན་བསྒྲུབ་ལ་སྐྱོ་ངལ་མེད་པར་ཤོག
རླབས་ཆེན་གཞན་དོན་ཕྱོགས་རིས་མེད་པ་ཡིས།
ཐམས་ཅད་ཕྲུམ་གཅིག་སངས་རྒྱས་ཐོབ་པར་ཤོག།

Colophon

རྫོགས་པ་ཆེན་པོ་ཀློང་ཆེན་སྙིང་ཐིག་གི་སྔོན་འགྲོའི་ངག་འདོན་ཁྲིགས་སུ་སྡེབས་པ་རྣམ་མཁྱེན་ལམ་བཟང་འདི་ཉིད་རིག་འཛིན་འཇིགས་མེད་གླིང་པ་སོགས་དམ་པ་དུ་མས་བཀའ་དྲིན་གྱིས་བསྐྱངས་ཤིང་དམ་ཚིག་ལ་མོས་པ་ཐོབ་པའི་སྔགས་ཀྱི་རྣལ་འབྱོར་པ་ཆེན་པོ་འཇིགས་མེད་ཕྲིན་ལས་འོད་ཟེར་གྱིས་བྲིས་པའི་དགེ་བས་རྗེས་འཇུག་རྣམས་ཀྱི་བླ་མ་སངས་རྒྱས་སུ་མཐོང་འགྲུབ་ཀྱིས་རང་རིག་ཀུན་ཏུ་བཟང་པོའི་རང་ཞལ་མངོན་དུ་གྱུར་ནས་འགྲོ་ཁམས་རྒྱ་མཚོ་ལ་ཕན་བརྒྱུད་ཚད་མེད་པའི་རྒྱུར་གྱུར་ཅིག།

Great Bliss Blazing

BY MIPHAM RINPOCHE

༄ སྣང་སྲིད་དབང་དུ་སྡུད་པའི་གསོལ་འདེབས་བྱིན་རླབས་སྤྲིན་ཆེན་བཞུགས་སོ།

ཨོཾ་ཨཱ་ཧཱུྃ་ཧྲཱིཿ

བདེ་ཆེན་འབར་བ་དབང་གི་ཕོ་བྲང་དུ།

བདེ་སྟོང་སོ་སོར་རྟོགས་པའི་ཡེ་ཤེས་སྐུ།

མ་ཆགས་བདེ་ལྡན་པདྨའི་རང་བཞིན་ལས།

རྡོ་རྗེ་ཉི་མ་སྣང་བ་ཆེན་པོའི་དཔལ།

ཆོས་སྐུ་སྣང་བ་མཐའ་ཡས་རྡོ་རྗེ་ཆོས།

འཇིག་རྟེན་དབང་ཕྱུག་ཐུགས་རྗེའི་རྗེས་ཆགས་གཟུགས།

པདྨ་རྒྱལ་པོ་འཁོར་འདས་མངའ་དབང་བསྒྱུར།

སྣང་སྲིད་ཟིལ་གནོན་དབང་ཆེན་ཧེ་རུ་ཀ

གསང་བ་ཡེ་ཤེས་བཛྲ་ཝ་ར་ཧི།

བདེ་མཆོག་འདོད་པའི་རྒྱལ་པོ་བདེ་ཆེན་གཏེར།

མ་ལུས་སྐྱེ་རྒྱུའི་ཡིད་འཕྲོག་རིག་བྱེད་མ།

མཆོག་ཐུན་ཕྱག་རྒྱའི་དབང་ཕྱུག་བདེ་སྟོང་གར།

དབང་མཛད་རྡོ་རྗེ་དཔའ་བོ་ཌཱ་ཀིའི་ཚོགས།

སྣང་སྟོང་མཉམ་པ་ཆེན་པོའི་ངང་ཉིད་དུ།

རྡོ་རྗེ་སྐུ་ཡི་གར་གྱིས་སྲིད་གསུམ་གཡོ།
འགགས་མེད་གསུང་གི་བཞད་སྒྲས་ཁམས་གསུམ་འགུགས།
འོད་ཟེར་དམར་པོ་འཁོར་འདས་ཡོངས་ལ་ཁྱབ།
སྲིད་ཞིའི་དྭངས་བཅུད་གཡོ་ཞིང་སྡུད་པར་བྱེད།
རྡོ་རྗེ་ཆགས་པ་ཆེན་པོའི་ཐུགས་ཀྱིས་ནི།
རྣམ་གཉིས་དངོས་གྲུབ་འདོད་རྒུའི་མཆོག་སྩོལ་ཞིང་།
རྡོ་རྗེ་ལྕགས་ཀྱུ་ཞགས་པ་ཆེན་པོ་ཡིས།
སྣང་སྲིད་བདེ་བ་ཆེན་པོར་སྡོམ་བྱེད་པ།
མཐའ་ཡས་སྤྲུལ་འཕྲུལ་དྲ་བའི་རོལ་གར་ཅན།
ཏིལ་གྱི་གོང་བུ་ཕྱེ་བ་བཞིན་བཞུགས་པའི།
རབ་འབྱམས་རྩ་གསུམ་དབང་གི་ལྷ་ཚོགས་ལ།
གུས་པས་གསོལ་བ་འདེབས་སོ་བྱིན་གྱིས་རློབས།
མཆོག་ཐུན་དངོས་གྲུབ་འདོད་རྒུའི་དཔལ་མཐའ་དག
ཐོགས་མེད་དབང་དུ་བྱེད་པའི་དངོས་གྲུབ་སྩོལ།

ཅེས་པའང་རབ་ཚེས་ས་ཡོས་ཟླ་ཚེས་ལ་ཧྲི་མིང་པས་སྤེལ།

Condensed Heart Essence:

A Close and Excellent Path to Enlightenment

BY ADZOM PAYLO RINPOCHE

ཀློང་ཆེན་སྙིང་གི་ཐིག་ལེ་ལས། སྔོན་འགྲོ་ཉེར་བསྡུས་བྱང་ཆུབ་ལམ་བཟང་བཞུགས།

Purification of Speech*

ན་མོ་གུ་རུ་བྷྱཿ

རླུང་རོ་དགུ་བསལ།	Nine Breathings
རླུང་བྱིན་རློབ།	Purification of Winds
ངག་བྱིན་རློབ།	Purification of Speech

* Jigme Lingpa's written text opens the recitation with the Lama Khyen invocation. Our version includes in writing the purification of breath, winds, and speech that in practice always precedes this invocation.

ཨོཾ་ཨཱ་ཧཱུྃ།
ལྷོ་དབང་ར་ཡིག་ལས་བྱུང་མེས་བསྲེགས་ནས།
འོད་དམར་རྣམ་པའི་ཪྫོ་ཛྫེ་ཏྟེ་གསུམ་སྦྱབས།
ཨཱ་ལི་ཀཱ་ལིའི་མཐའ་སྐོར་རྟེན་འབྲེལ་སྙིང༌།
སུ་ཧྲིག་ཕྲེང་བ་ལྷ་བུའི་ཡིག་འབྲུ་ལས།
འོད་འཕྲོས་རྒྱལ་བ་སྲས་བཅས་མཆོད་པས་མཉེས།
སླར་འདུས་ངག་སྒྲིབ་དག་ནས་གསུང་ཪྫོ་ཛྫེའི།
བྱིན་རླབས་དངོས་གྲུབ་ཐམས་ཅད་ཐོབ་པར་བསམ།
ཨ་ཨཱ། ཨི་ཨཱི། ཨུ་ཨཱུ། རི་རཱི། ལི་ལཱི། ཨེ་ཨཻ། ཨོ་ཨཽ། ཨཾ་ཨཿ
ཀ་ཁ་ག་གྷ་ང༌། ཙ་ཚ་ཛ་ཛྷ་ཉ། ཊ་ཋ་ཌ་ཌྷ་ཎ། ཏ་ཐ་ད་དྷ་ན།
པ་ཕ་བ་བྷ་མ། ཡ་ར་ལ་ཝ། ཤ་ཥ་ས་ཧ་ཀྵ།
ཡེ་དྷརྨཱ་ཧེ་ཏུ་པྲ་བྷ་ཝཱ་ཧེ་ཏུན་ཏེ་ཥཱན་ཐཱ་ག་ཏོ་ཧྱ་ཝ་དཏ།
ཏེ་ཥཱཉྩ་ཡོ་ནི་རོ་དྷ་ཨེ་ཝཾ་བཱ་དཱི་མ་ཧཱ་ཤྲ་མ་ཎ་སྭཱ་ཧཱ།*

CALLING THE LAMA

བླ་མ་མཁྱེན། བླ་མ་མཁྱེན། བླ་མ་མཁྱེན། ལན་གསུམ།
སྙིང་དབུས་དད་པའི་གེ་སར་བཞད་པ་ནས།
སྐྱབས་གཅིག་དྲིན་ཆེན་བླ་མ་ཡར་ལ་བཞེངས།
ལས་དང་ཉོན་མོངས་དྲག་པོས་གཟིར་བ་ཡི།
སྐལ་པ་ངན་པ་བདག་ལ་སྐྱོབ་པའི་ཕྱིར།
སྤྱི་བོར་བདེ་ཆེན་འཁོར་ལོའི་རྒྱན་དུ་བཞུགས།
དྲན་དང་ཤེས་བཞིན་ཀུན་ཀྱང་བཞེངས་སུ་གསོལ།

* Due to a font issue, the mantra incorrectly reads *nytsa* when it should actually read *nyca*.

དལ་འབྱོར་རྙེད་དཀའ་དོན་མེད་གཡེང་བས་བསླུས།
མི་རྟག་འཆི་བར་རྟག་འཛིན་བློ་ཡིས་འཆིང་།
ལས་འབྲས་བསླུ་མེད་ཉོན་མོངས་གཞན་དབང་ཤོར།
སྡུག་བསྔལ་འཁོར་བར་ཡིད་བསླུས་གྱུར་པ་བདག
མྱུར་དུ་སྐྱབས་གཅིག་བླ་མ་ཐུགས་རྗེ་ཅན།
བློ་སྣ་བསྒྱུར་གཅིག་བླ་མ་བཀའ་དྲིན་ཅན།
དལ་རྟེན་དོན་ལྡན་མི་རྟག་རྒྱུད་བསྐུལ་ཞིང་།
རྣམ་དག་ཁྲིམས་བསྲུང་འཁོར་བར་ཡིད་དབྱུང་ཤོག

I. Refuge སྐྱབས་འགྲོ་ནི།

དཀོན་མཆོག་གསུམ་དངོས་བདེ་གཤེགས་རྩ་བ་གསུམ༔
རྩ་རླུང་ཐིག་ལེའི་རང་བཞིན་བྱང་ཆུབ་སེམས༔
ངོ་བོ་རང་བཞིན་ཐུགས་རྗེའི་དཀྱིལ་འཁོར་ལ༔
བྱང་ཆུབ་སྙིང་པོའི་བར་དུ་སྐྱབས་སུ་མཆི༔ ལན་གསུམ།

II. Bodhicitta Motivation སེམས་བསྐྱེད་ནི།

ཧོ༔ སྣ་ཚོགས་སྣང་བ་ཆུ་ཟླའི་རྫུན་རིས་ཀྱིས༔
འཁོར་བ་ལུ་གུ་རྒྱུད་དུ་འཁྱམས་པའི་འགྲོ༔
རང་རིག་འོད་གསལ་དབྱིངས་སུ་ངལ་གསོའི་ཕྱིར༔
ཚད་མེད་བཞི་ཡི་ངང་ནས་སེམས་བསྐྱེད་དོ༔ ལན་གསུམ། *[3 times]*

III. Vajrasattva རྡོ་རྗེ་སེམས་པ།

ཨཱཿ བདག་ཉིད་སྤྱི་བོར་པད་ཟླའི་སྟེང་།
ཧཱུྃ་ལས་བླ་མ་རྡོ་རྗེ་སེམས།
དཀར་གསལ་རྡོ་དྲིལ་རྒྱན་ཆས་སྤྲས།
ཡབ་ཡུམ་ཐུགས་ཀའི་ཟླ་དཀྱིལ་ཧཱུྃ།
བསྐོར་བའི་སྔགས་ལས་བདུད་རྩིའི་རྒྱུན།
བབས་པས་ནད་གདོན་སྡིག་སྒྲིབ་སྦྱངས།

HUNDRED-SYLLABLE MANTRA ཡི་གེ་བརྒྱ་པ་བཟློད།

ཨོཾ་བཛྲ་སཏྭ་ས་མ་ཡ། མ་ནུ་པཱ་ལ་ཡ།
བཛྲ་སཏྭ་ཏྭེ་ནོ་པ། ཏིཥྛ་དྲི་ཌྷོ་མེ་བྷ་ཝ།
སུ་ཏོཥྱོ་མེ་བྷ་ཝ། སུ་པོཥྱོ་མེ་བྷ་ཝ།
ཨ་ནུ་རཀྟོ་མེ་བྷ་ཝ།སརྦ་སིདྡྷི་མྨེ་པྲ་ཡཙྪ།
སརྦ་ཀརྨ་སུ་ཙ་མེ། ཙིཏྟཾ་ཤྲེ་ཡཾཿཀུ་རུ་ཧཱུྃ།
ཧ་ཧ་ཧ་ཧ་ཧོ། བྷ་ག་ཝཱན། སརྦ་ཏ་ཐཱ་ག་ཏ།
བཛྲ་མཱ་མེ་མུཉྩ། བཛྲཱི་བྷ་ཝ་མ་ཧཱ་ས་མ་ཡ་ས་ཏྭ་ཨཱཿཧཱུྃ་ཕཊ༔
རྡོར་སེམས་འོད་ཞུ་རང་ལ་ཐིམ།
སྣོད་བཅུད་སྐུ་དང་ཞིང་ཁམས་གྱུར།

SIX-SYLLABLE MANTRA ཡི་དྲུག་བཟློད།

ཨོཾ་བཛྲ་ས་ཏྭ་ཧཱུྃ༔

IV. Mandala མཎྜལ།

ཨོཾ་ཨཱ་ཧཱུྃ༔

སྐུ་གསུམ་ཞིང་ཁམས་རྒྱ་མཚོ་རྡུལ་གཅིག་གིས།

ཕྲ་རབ་རེ་རེའི་ཁོངས་སུ་རྡུལ་སྙེད་གྲངས།

དཔག་མེད་བློས་བླང་སྐྱབས་གནས་རྒྱ་མཚོ་ལ།

འབུལ་ལོ་ཚོགས་རྫོགས་དོན་གཉིས་ལྷུན་གྲུབ་ཤོག

ཨི་དཾ་གུ་རུ་རཏྣ་མཎྜལ་ཀཾ་ནི་རྱཱ་ཏ་ཡཱ་མི།།

V. Severance གཅོད།

ཕཊ༔

རང་རིག་ཡུམ་ཆེན་ངོ་བོ་དབྱིངས་སུ་སྤར༔

བདག་འཛིན་སྒྱུ་ལུས་འདོད་ཡོན་ཚོགས་སུ་གཤམ༔

མཆོད་སྦྱིན་མགྲོན་རྣམས་ཅི་བདེར་ལྷག་མེད་བཞེས༔

ཟག་མེད་ཆོས་སྐུའི་དགོངས་པ་མངོན་གྱུར་ཤོག༔

ཕཊ༔

VI. Guru Yoga བླ་མའི་རྣལ་འབྱོར།

ཨེ་མ་ཧོ༔

རང་སྣང་ཟང་མདོག་དཔལ་རིའི་དབུས།

བདག་ཉིད་རྡོ་རྗེ་རྣལ་འབྱོར་མའི།

སྤྱི་བོར་པདྨ་ཉི་ཟླའི་སྟེང་།

བླ་མ་དབྱེར་མེད་པདྨ་འབྱུང་།

བརྡ་དོན་རྟགས་ཀྱི་ཆས་རྫོགས་བཞུགས།

རྩ་གསུམ་རིག་འཛིན་རྒྱ་མཚོས་བསྐོར།

སྣང་སྟོང་མཉམ་གནས་ཆེན་པོར་གསལ།

ཧཱུྃ༔

ཨོ་རྒྱན་ཡུལ་གྱི་ནུབ་བྱང་མཚམས༔

པདྨ་གེ་སར་སྡོང་པོ་ལ༔

ཡ་མཚན་མཆོག་གི་དངོས་གྲུབ་བརྙེས༔

པདྨ་འབྱུང་གནས་ཞེས་སུ་གྲགས༔

འཁོར་དུ་མཁའ་འགྲོ་མང་པོས་བསྐོར༔

ཁྱེད་ཀྱི་རྗེས་སུ་བདག་བསྒྲུབ་ཀྱིས༔

བྱིན་གྱིས་བརླབ་ཕྱིར་གཤེགས་སུ་གསོལ༔

གུ་རུ་པདྨ་སིདྡྷི་ཧཱུྃ༔

THE SEVEN-BRANCH PUJA

ཧྲཱིཿ གུས་པས་ཕྱག་འཚལ་མཆོད་པ་འབུལ།

སྡིག་བཤགས་དགེ་ལ་རྗེས་ཡི་རང་།

ཆོས་འཁོར་བསྐོར་ནས་རྟག་བརྟན་བཞུགས།

དགེ་ཚོགས་འོད་གསལ་དབྱིངས་སུ་བསྔོ། ལན་གསུམ། *[3 times]*

སྐྱབས་གནས་ཀུན་འདུས་མ་ཧ་གུ་རུ

བཟོད་མེད་གདུང་བས་སྙིང་ནས་འབོད་ན།

བདག་ལ་ཐུགས་རྗེའི་སྤྱན་གྱིས་གཟིགས་ནས།

བྱིན་རླབས་དབང་བསྐུར་ད་ལྟ་སྩོལ་ཅིག ལན་གསུམ། *[3 times]*

བསྙེན་པ་བཛྲ་གུ་རུ་ལ་འབད།

ཨོཾ་ཨཱཿཧཱུྃ་བཛྲ་གུ་རུ་པདྨ་སིདྡྷི་ཧཱུྃ༔

VII. Prayers to the Lineage Lamas

ཨེ་མ་ཧོཿ

ཀུན་བཟང་རྡོར་སེམས་དགའ་རབ་ཤྲཱི་སེང་།

འཇམ་དཔལ་གཤེས་གཉེན་ཛྙཱ་ན་སུ་ཏྲ་དང་།

བི་མ་པད་འབྱུང་ཐུགས་སྲས་རྗེ་གྲོགས་འབངས།

ཀློང་ཆེན་རབ་འབྱམས་རིག་འཛིན་འཇིགས་མེད་གླིང་།

ཀུན་བཟང་གཞན་ཕན་རྒྱལ་བའི་མྱུ་གུ་དང་།

དྲི་མེད་བློ་གྲོས་རྡོ་རྗེ་གཟི་བརྗིད་རྩལ།

དྲི་མེད་ཀློང་ཡངས་འགྱུར་མེད་རྡོ་རྗེ་དང་།

པདྨ་དབང་རྒྱལ་པདྨ་ཕྲིན་ལས་རྗེ།

ཀརྨ་བཛྲ་ཐུབ་བསྟན་རྒྱ་མཚོ་ལ།

གསོལ་བ་འདེབས་སོ་དོན་གཉིས་ལྷུན་གྲུབ་ཤོག

བླ་མའི་གནས་གསུམ་གྱི་ཡིག་འབྲུ་གསུམ་ལས་འོད་ཟེར་དཀར་དམར་མཐིང་གསུམ་རིམ་དང་ཅིག་

ཆར་དུ་བྱུང་།

རང་གི་གནས་གསུམ་དུ་རིམ་དང་ཅིག་ཆར་དུ་ཐིམ་པས།

སྐུ་གསུང་ཐུགས་ཀྱི་དམ་ཚིག་ཉམས་ཆག་དག། བྱིན་རླབས་ཞུགས་དབང་བཞི་ཐོབ།

སྒྲིབ་བཞི་སྦྱངས།

རིག་འཛིན་བཞིའི་ས་བོན་ཐེབས། སྐུ་བཞིའི་གོ་འཕང་གི་སྐལ་བ་རྒྱུད་ལ་བཞག་གོ

ཐུགས་ཡིད་བསྲེས་དང་བསྙེན་པ་ཡིད་བཟླས་བྱ།

བླ་མ་འོད་ཞུ་རང་ལ་ཐིམ་མ་བཅོས་ལྷུན་གྲུབ་ཆེན་པོར་

ཨཿ ཨཿ ཨཿ

Close-Lineage Prayer

རིག་པ་འཛིན་པ་འགྱུར་མེད་རྡོ་རྗེ་དང་།
རྒྱལ་བའི་སྲས་པོ་པདྨ་དབང་གི་རྒྱལ།
རྗེ་བཙུན་ཀུན་བཟང་འཆི་མེད་དབང་མོ་བཅས།
གསོལ་བ་འདེབས་སོ་ཉམས་ལེན་མཐར་ཕྱིན་ཤོག

ཅེས་འགྱུར་མེད་རྡོ་རྗེས་བྲིས་པ་དགེ།

Sharing the Merit (*Three Dedication Prayers*)

དགེ་བ་འདི་ཡིས་མྱུར་དུ་བདག
མ་ཧཱ་གུ་རུ་འགྲུབ་གྱུར་ནས།
འགྲོ་བ་གཅིག་ཀྱང་མ་ལུས་པ།
དེ་ཡི་ས་ལ་འགོད་པར་ཤོག
སྐྱེ་བ་ཀུན་ཏུ་ཡང་དག་བླ་མ་དང་།
འབྲལ་མེད་ཆོས་ཀྱི་དཔལ་ལ་ལོངས་སྤྱོད་ནས།
ས་དང་ལམ་གྱི་ཡོན་ཏན་རབ་རྫོགས་ཏེ།
རྡོ་རྗེ་འཆང་གི་གོ་འཕང་མྱུར་ཐོབ་ཤོག
ཐུབ་བསྟན་མཛེས་པའི་རྒྱན་གཅིག་ཀློང་ཆེན་པ།
བཤད་སྒྲུབ་བསྟན་པའི་མངའ་བདག་འཇིགས་མེད་གླིང་།
མཚུངས་མེད་བླ་མའི་བསྟན་པ་སྲིད་མཐའི་བར།
བཤད་སྒྲུབ་ཐོས་བསམ་སྒོམ་པས་འཛིན་གྱུར་ཅིག

Colophon

ཅེས་པ་འདི་ནི་མདོ་སྔགས་ཐེག་པ་ཀུན་དང་མཐུན་ཅིང་ཀུན་ལས་ཉེ་ལམ་རྨད་དུ་བྱུང་བ་འོད་གསལ་རྫོགས་པ་ཆེན་པོའི་ལམ་བཟང་རིག་འཛིན་འཇིགས་མེད་གླིང་པའི་རང་བྱུང་དགོངས་པའི་ཀློང་ནས་རྡོལ་བའི་ཟབ་གསང་རྡོ་རྗེའི་ཚིག་ལ་བདག་འདྲ་སོ་སྐྱེས་དབྱེ་བསྡུས་སྦྱོབ་པ་དང་བྲལ་ཞིང་། ཕྱིན་ཀློབ་

ཉམས་པའི་རྒྱུར་གྱུར་པས་སྙིགས་ནས་གནོང་འགྱོད་འཆིས་མོད། འོན་ཏེ་སྙིགས་དུས་འདིར་ཉོན་མོངས་དང་ལེ་ལོའི་དབང་བཙན་པས་དགེ་སྦྱོང་གྱི་ན་བ་འགགས་བགྱིད་ལུགས་པར་མི་འགྱུར་བའི་ཕྱིར་འདི་ལྟར་དགོས་ཞེས་ལམ་འདི་ལ་མོས་པའི་དད་ལྡན་སློབ་མ་ཨ་རིའི་སློབ་གྲྭའི་དགེ་རྒན་ཆེན་མོ་ཨ་ནེ་ཁེ་ལན་ནམ་ཆོས་མིང་རིག་འཛིན་སྒྲོལ་མ་སོགས་སློབ་བུ་དུ་མས་ཡང་ཡང་ནན་དུ་བསྐུལ་ངོར། ཨ་རིའི་ཤར་ལྷོའི་གྲོང་ཁྱེར་ཏུས་སུ་གྲོན་ནས་ཨ་འཛོམ་སྤྲུལ་མིང་དུ་འབོད་པ་འགྱུར་མེད་ཐུབ་བསྟན་རྒྱ་མཚོས་ཀློང་སྙིང་སྔོན་འགྲོའི་གཞུང་དང་། དམ་པ་དུ་མའི་གསུང་ལ་གཞི་བྱས་རང་བློར་གང་དཔོག་སུ་བྲིས་པའི་ཉེས་པ་འཆིས་ན་རྩ་གསུམ་ལྷ་ལ་བཤགས་ཞིང་། ལེགས་པའི་དགེ་བས་འགྲོ་ཀུན་རིག་འཛིན་བླ་མས་རྗེས་སུ་འཛིན་པའི་རྒྱུར་གྱུར་ཅིག སརྦ་མངྒ་ལཾ།

Further Prayers

These can be linked with any practice session.

LONG-LIFE PRAYER FOR ADZOM GYALSE PAYLO RINPOCHE

ཨོཾ་སྭསྟི༔

བསླུ་མེད་སྐྱབས་གནས་རྒྱ་མཚོའི་མཐུ་བྱིན་གྱིས།

བསྟན་འགྲོའི་མགོན་དཔུང་དྲིན་ཆེན་ཆོས་ཀྱི་རྗེ།

འགྱུར་མེད་ཐུབ་བསྟན་རྒྱ་མཚོ་དཔལ་བཟང་པོ།

ཞབས་པད་བརྟན་ཅིང་མཛད་ཕྲིན་ཀུན་ཁྱབ་ཤོག།

ཅེས་གསུམ་སློབ་དགེ་བས་གསོལ་བ་བཏབས་།

RECITATION AFTER DEDICATION

སྣང་གྲགས་རིག་གསུམ་ལྷ་སྔགས་ཆོས་སྐུའི་ངང་།

སྐུ་དང་ཡེ་ཤེས་རོལ་པར་འབྱམས་ཀླས་པར།

ཟབ་གསང་རྣལ་འབྱོར་ཆེན་པོའི་ཉམས་ལེན་ལ།

དབྱེར་མེད་ཐུགས་ཀྱི་ཐིག་ལེར་རོ་གཅིག་ཤོག

PRAYER TO THE *HEART ESSENCE* (*NYINGTHIG*) PROTECTORS

སྙིང་ཐིག་གསོལ་བསྐུལ་བཞུགས།

ཧཱུྃ༔

དཔལ་ལྡན་ཨེ་ཀ་ཛ་ཊི་དང་།

དྲང་སྲོང་ཁྱབ་འཇུག་ར་ཧུ་ལ།

དམ་ཅན་རྡོ་རྗེ་ལེགས་པ་སོགས།

སྙིང་ཐིག་གཉེན་པོའི་བསྟན་སྲུང་ཚོགས།

དམ་རྫས་བདུད་རྩིའི་གཏོར་མ་འབུལ།

རྣལ་འབྱོར་བདག་ལ་མགོན་སྐྱོབ་མཛོད།

བཅོལ་བའི་ཕྲིན་ལས་མ་གཡེལ་སྒྲུབས།

ཞེས་མ་དགོན་བླ་མ་གཞན་ཕན་ཐུགས་བཞེད་ལྟར་ཕུལ་བ་དགེ།

FAITHFUL STUDENT SONG

སློབ་མ་རྣམ་ངེས་འབྱུང་བསྐུལ་བའི་གཏམ་ཐར་ལམ་བཟང་པོ་བཞུགས།།

ADVICE EXHORTING STUDENTS TO LEAVE SAMSARA BEHIND: AN EXCELLENT PATH TO LIBERATION

དཀོན་མཆོག་རིན་ཆེན་རྣམ་གསུམ།

གདུང་བས་སྙིང་ནས་འབོད་ན།

ཐུགས་རྗེས་སྤྱན་གྱིས་གཟིགས་རོགས།

རེ་ས་གཞན་ན་མེད་དོ།

ཐོབ་དཀའ་མི་ཡི་ལུས་རྟེན།

མི་རྟག་ཐོག་བབས་སྒྲིབ་ཚེ།

འཆི་བྲོད་གདིང་ཆེན་ཡི་ཡོད།

དད་ལྡན་བསྐལ་བཟང་སློབ་མ།
ལྷ་འདུས་ཕུང་ལྷའི་ཚོགས་པ།
ནམ་ཞིག་བློ་གཏད་མི་འདུག
སྙིང་ནས་འཆི་བར་བསམ་ཤིག
དད་ལྡན་བསྐལ་བཟང་སློབ་མ།
ལས་འབྲས་བསླུ་མེད་ཡིན་པས།
མི་དགེའི་རྟོག་པ་སྤྱང་ཞིང་།
ལྷ་ཆོས་དགེ་བ་བརྩོན་རོག
དད་ལྡན་བསྐལ་བཟང་སློབ་མ།
འཁོར་བ་སྒྱུ་མའི་བསླུ་བྲིད།
ཡིད་སེམས་ཆགས་པ་མེད་པར།
ད་རེས་ཐར་ལམ་བྲོས་ཤོག
དད་ལྡན་བསྐལ་བཟང་སློབ་མ།
བློ་རྩེ་གཉིས་སུ་མེད་པའི།
ལྡོག་མེད་མོས་གུས་ཡོད་ན།
ཕྱི་མ་བླ་སློབ་མཉམ་འགྲོ།
དད་ལྡན་བསྐལ་བཟང་སློབ་མ།
འགྱུར་མེད་ཐུབ་བསྟན་རྒྱ་མཚོ།
སྙིང་ནས་བླ་མར་འདོད་ན།
གདམས་ངག་དེ་ལྷག་མེད་དོ།
སྙིང་གཏམ་སྙིང་ལ་བཅུག་རོག
ཨ་ཧོ་ཨ་ལ་ལ་ཧོ།
ཨ་མཚར་མཚར་སྒྱུ་འཕྲུལ་ཡོད།
ཨ་ཧོ་ཨ་ལ་ལ་ཧོ།
ཨ་མཚར་མཚར་སྒྱུ་འཕྲུལ་ཡོད།

Threefold Epilogue

BY KHETSUN SANGPO RINPOCHE

༄༅། ཀྱེ་ལགས། ཟབ་མོ་སྔགས་ཀྱི་ལམ་བཟང་བགྲོད་འདོད་ན་མེད་དུ་མི་རུང་བ་ནི། ཕྱི་ནང་གསང་གསུམ་གྱི་སྔོན་འགྲོའི་ཆོས་རྣམས་ལ་ནན་ཏན་མཛད་དགོས་པ་དེ་རེད། དེ་ལྟར་མཛད་ཚེ། འགོ་དང་པོ་ནས་མ་འཆུག་པ་ཡིན་ཙ་ན། དངོས་གཞིའི་ཆོས་རྣམས་ལའང་རྒྱུ་ཕུན་ཚོགས་ལ་བརྟེན་ནས་འབྲས་བུ་ཕུན་སུམ་ཚོགས་པ་ཡོང་བ་སློས་མ་དགོས་པ་ལྟ་བུ་རེད་ཅེས། དེ་སྐད་ཁྱེད་ཀྱི་རེ་འདོད་བསྐོང་ཕྱིར་དུ། ཐག་རིང་ཡུལ་ནས་ཞུ་ཚིག་བྲུ་མ་ཏྲ། ཉིད་ཀྱི་དགེ་རྒན་རྒས་བུ་གང་ཉིད་ཀྱི་སྙིང་གཏམ་ཡིན་ནོ་སྙིང་ལ་བཅིངས་མཛོད་དང་། གདམས་ངག་ཡིན་ནོ་ཉམས་སུ་ལེན་མཛོད་ཅིག་ཅེས་སོ།།

. . . .

༄༅། ཆོས་དབྱིངས་མཁའ་ལྟར་དག་པའི་དབྱིངས་ཉིད་ལ།
སྒྱུ་འཕྲུལ་ཞི་ཁྲོའི་ལྷ་ཚོགས་རབ་འབྱམས་ཀྱིས།
ཐུགས་རྗེ་ཚད་མེད་གདུལ་བྱའི་ཞིང་ཀུན་ཏུ།
གང་ལ་གང་གདུལ་ཕྲིན་ལས་བསམ་མི་ཁྱབ།
འབྲེལ་ཚད་དོན་ལྡན་མཛད་པ་མཐའ་ཡས་སོ།
བདག་སོགས་བྲིས་པའི་བསམ་བརྗོད་ཡུལ་ལས་འདས།

ཨེ་མ།

ཆོས་ཀྱི་ཕུང་པོའི་དོན་གྱི་སྙིང་པོ་ཀུན།

འདུས་ནས་མན་ངག་སྟོན་འགྲོའི་ཆོས་རྣམས་གསུངས།

དེ་ལ་བརྟེན་ནས་བྱས་བསགས་སྡིག་ལྟུང་ཀུན།

སྦྱང་ནས་མ་ནོར་ལམ་བཟང་འདི་ལས་གཞན།

མེད་ཅེས་དམ་པའི་གསུང་ལ་ཡིད་ལས་གཞན།

མེད་ཅེས་དམ་པའི་གསུང་ལ་ཡིད་ཆེས་ནས།

ལམ་བཟང་འདི་ཉིད་འགྱུར་ཞུས་གདན་ལ་ཕབ།།

. . . .

རིག་པས་གསལ་ཞིང་ལུང་གི་མཐའ་ནས་བརྟེན།

དོན་གྱི་སྙིང་པོ་ཚིག་གི་ཕྲེང་བར་བལྟར།

གནས་ལུགས་དག་ལ་ཡང་ཡང་གཟིགས་ཆེད་དུ།

སྟོན་གྱི་དབང་པོར་ཞུ་མཆིས་ལགས་སོ་ཀྱེ།

. . . .

ཨཊིའི་སྒྲུབ་བརྒྱུད་ཡོངས་ཀྱི་བརྟེན་གནས་ཆེ།

གཙུག་ལག་ཁང་ཆེན་གསར་དུ་ཆོས་པ་ཡི།

ཕྱོགས་ཀྱི་མཐའ་གྲུ་ཀུན་ཏུ་ཁྱབ་གྱུར་ནས།

ཡུལ་ཕྱོགས་ཐམས་ཅད་རྣལ་འབྱོར་ཕོ་མོ་ཡི།

ཁྱབ་ནས་བསྟན་ལ་བྱ་བ་བྱེད་པར་ཤོག

—Khetsun Sangpo Rinpoche

A prayer for Dawn Mountain and the flourishing of the Dharma, inspired and composed in Houston on September 15, 2003, at dawn.

Bibliography and Suggested Readings

Books

Dudjom Rinpoche, Jikdrel Yeshe Dorje. 1991. *The Nyingma School of Tibetan Buddhism: Its Fundamentals and History.* Trans. and ed. Gyurme Dorje with the collaboration of Matthew Kapstein. Boston: Wisdom Publications. An encyclopedic treasure in two volumes.

Germano, David. 1992. "Poetic Thought, the Intelligent Universe, and the Mystery of Self: The Tantric Synthesis of rDzogs Chen in Fourteenth-Century Tibet." Ph.D. dissertation, University of Wisconsin.

Goodman, Steven D. 1983. "The *kLong-chen sNying Thig*: An Eighteenth-Century Tibetan Revelation." Ph.D. dissertation, University of Saskatchewan.

Gyatso, Janet. 1998. *Apparitions of the Self: The Secret Biographies of a Tibetan Visionary*. Princeton, NJ: Princeton University Press. Translation and close reading of Jigme Lingpa's work and life.

Gyurme Tsering, ed. and photographer. 2006. *Earth Thunder: Stories from the Life of Adzom Paylo Rinpoche*. Chengdu, China.

Klein, Anne Carolyn. 1996. *Meeting the Great Bliss Queen: Buddhists, Feminists and the Art of the Self.* Boston: Beacon Press. Background on Yeshe Tsogyal, the leading female figure of the *Longchen Nyingthig* tradition in the context of cross-cultural reflections. Reprinted 2008 by Snow Lion Publications.

Klein, Anne Carolyn, and Geshe Tenzin Wangyal Rinpoche. 2006. *Unbounded Wholeness: Dzogchen, Bon, and the Logic of the Nonconceptual.* New York: Oxford University Press. Translation and study of an early Dzogchen text in the Bön tradition, laying out why *rigpa* is not mind in philosophical terms very similar to those of Mipham Rinpoche in *Fundamental Mind* and Dudjom Rinpoche in *History*; authenticity of open awareness.

Namkhai Norbu Rinpoche, Chögyal. 2000. *The Crystal and the Way of Light.* Comp. John Shane. Ithaca, NY: Snow Lion Publications. Part autobiography and all inspiration.

———. 2006. *Dzogchen Teachings.* Ithaca, NY: Snow Lion Publications. A compilation of practical instructions for meditation.

Patrul Rinpoche. 1994. *The Words of My Perfect Teacher* (*Kun zang bla ma'i she lung*). Trans. Padmakara Translation Group. San Francisco: HarperCollins. The classic commentary on the foundational practices, beloved by all Tibetan traditions.

Pelzang, Khenpo Ngawang. 2004. *A Guide to* The Words of My Perfect Teacher. Boston: Shambhala.

Sangpo, Khetsun Rinpoche. 1982. *Tantric Practice in Nyingma.* Trans. Jeffrey Hopkins. Ithaca, NY: Snow Lion Publications. Instructions on practicing Jigme Lingpa's *Heart Essence.*

Thondup, Tulku. 1984. *The Tantric Tradition of the Nyingmapa.* Marion, MA.: Buddhayana Foundation. An essential source for history of the tradition.

———. 1995. *Enlightened Journey: Buddhist Practice as Daily Life.* Ed. Harold Talbott. Boston and London: Shambhala. Background on Nyingma practice and ritual that pertains also to the foundational practices.

———. 1996. *The Practice of Dzogchen.* Ithaca, NY: Snow Lion Publications. An indispensable resource.

———. 1999. *Masters of Meditation and Miracles.* Boston: Shambhala. Short biographies of exemplars in the *Longchen Nyingthig* lineage. For a list of the main texts and commentaries on the *Longchen Nyingthig,* Tibetan and English, see note 56, p. 362ff.

———. 2001. *The Dzogchen: Innermost Essence Preliminary Practice.* Ed. Brian C. Beresford. New Delhi: Paljor Publications.

Articles

Germano, David. 1994. "Architecture and Absence in the Secret Tantric History of Tibet." *Journal of the International Association of Buddhist Studies* 17 (2): 203–335.

Goodman, Steven D. 1992. "Rig 'dzin 'Jigs-med gling-pa and the kLong-Chen sNying Thig." In *Tibetan Buddhism: Reason and Revelation*, ed. Steven Goodman and Ronald Davidson. Albany, NY: SUNY Press. Concisely presented details of Jigme Lingpa's life and work.

Kapstein, Matthew. 2000. "The Mark of Vermilion: Rebirth and Resurrection in an Early Medieval Tale." In *The Tibetan Assimilation of Buddhism*. New York: Oxford University Press.

Tibetan Texts

Adzom Drukpa. 1976. *A Lamp to Light Our Way: Instructions on the Foundational Practices of* Heart Essence, the Vast Expanse (*kLong chen snying thig gi sngon 'gro'i khrid yig thar lam gsal byed sgron me*). Damchoe Monlam, Chitra Monastery, Ballimaran, Delhi: Minali Jayyed Press. Available digitally through the Tibetan Buddhist Resource Center, New York.

Chökyi Dragpa. *Word Commentary/Word Commentary on the Recitation of the Foundational Practices for Heart Essence, the Vast Expanse, Lighting the Path to Omniscience* (*kLong chen snying thig gi sngon 'gro'i ngag 'don gyi 'bru 'grel rnam mkhyen lam sgron*). Chögyi Dragpa, also known as Khenpo Chodrag, may be the only surviving disciple of the great Khenpo Zhenga (mKhan po gzhan dga') of Dzogchen Monastery. Since at least the 1980s he has lived near Lhagang (Lhagon) (between Kanding [aka Tartsedo/Tachinlu] and Trago and Kandze) in Kham. As this manuscript was being completed, word came that he had passed on.

Jamyang Khyentse Wangpo. 1966. *kLong chen snying tig gi sngon 'gro'i ngag 'don rnam mkhyen lam bzang gsal byed*. Gangtok: sNgags rigs 'dzin pa hal po chos grags. 25 folios.

Jigme Lingpa. *Thun mong gi sngon-'gro khrid kyi lag len la 'debs lugs. Collected Works*, vol. 8, pp. 861–903. Reprinted in the *Nyingthig rtsa pod*, Dilgo Khyentse edition, vol. *hum*, pp. 237–70.

———. *Thun mong ma yin pa'i sngon 'gro'i khrid yig dran pa nyer gzhag. Collected Works*, vol. 8, pp. 905–43. Reprinted in the *Nyingthig rtsa pod*, Dilgo Khyentse edition, vol. *hum*, pp. 271–304.

———. *Thun mong dang thun mong ma yin pa'i sngon 'gro sangs ngag don thor bu'i skor*. In *Longchen Nyingthig*. Reprinted in the *Nyingthig rtsa pod*, Dilgo Khyentse edition, vol. *hum*, p. 647.

———. *Phyi sgrub bla ma'i rnal 'byor yid bzhin nor bu*. Reprinted in the *Nyingthig rtsa pod*, Dilgo Khyentse edition, vol. *om*, p. 133.

Jigme Thrinle Ozer (the First Dodrupchen). *rNam mkhyen lam bzang/ rDzogs pa chen po kLong chen sNying thig gi sNgon 'gro'i ngag 'don khrigs su sdebs pa rnam mkhyen lam bzang* in *The Collected Works of Kun mkhyen 'Jigs-med gling pa*, vol. 7 (*ja*), pp. 237–65.

Khetsun Sangpo Rinpoche. 1973. *Bibliographical Dictionary of Tibet and Tibetan Buddhism*. Vol. 4: The rNying-ma-pa Tradition. Dharamsala: Library of Tibetan Works and Archives.

Contributors

Adzom Paylo Rinpoche, Tibet/China

Born in 1971 near Chamdo, Adzom Rinpoche was soon named a *tulku* of the great scholar Gyalse Pema Wangyal, son of Adzom Drukpa Drodul Pao Dorje, by the abbot of his monastery. He is widely regarded as an incarnation of Jigme Lingpa.

Rinpoche is a lineage-holder of both the Mahamudra and Dzogchen lineages. In addition to teaching extensively from the *Longchen Nyingthig* in his home area, he also teaches from the body of treasures that are considered the "child" of the *Heart Essence, the Vast Essence,* the revelations of Adzom Drukpa known as *Secret Treasures of the Luminous Secret Vajra* (*'Od gsal rdo rje gzang mdzod*). In addition, he teaches more and more often from his own *ter.*

Jetsun Kacho Wangmo/Ani Sherab Chozo, Tibet/China

Recognized by many lamas in Tibet as an incarnation of Samantabhadri, Tara, Yeshe Tsogyal, Machig Lapdron, and others, Jetsunma left her home in eastern Tibet for a monastic college when she was seven years old. She began a rigorous study of Buddhism's texts, an education rarely available to women in that area at that time. At thirteen, she took vows and became a nun. She has nearly attained the highly respected degree of *khenpo,* and is deeply committed to making nuns' training available as widely as possible. She is the sister of Adzom Rinpoche and was his sister in their previous lives when they were the children of Adzom Drukpa and Ma Yum Tashi Hlamo.

Since early childhood, Jetsunma has had visions of Green Tara. "This just gets stronger," she has said. "It brings forth a lot of joy and a lot of bliss. My hope is that students will have the same joy and the same bliss." In Tibet, she is called upon to sing at monastic rituals and initiations, when hundreds and often thousands of monks and nuns sit by in prayer. Those who have been graced by the sound of her voice never forget its radiant purity. Her presence shines in the same way, which is why everyone loves her. Her CDs, taped in Chengdu, are available through Dawn Mountain.

Khetsun Sangpo Rinpoche, Sundarijal, Nepal

One of the very few remaining lamas who completed his esoteric training in traditional Tibet, Khetsun Sangpo Rinpoche received *Longchen Nyingthig* transmission in Tibet from Jetsun Shugsep and was a close student of the deeply revered cave-dwelling hermit Lama Gompo. In the Kathmandu Valley of Nepal he is one of the leading figures of the Ancient (Nyingma) School of Tibetan Buddhism. He is also the founder and main teacher of the Dudjom Center/Nyingma Monastery in Nepal, where he has trained several generations of monastic and *ngakpa* scholars. A consummate scholar as well as a great lineage practitioner, Khetsun Rinpoche has been a Visiting Scholar numerous times at both the University of Virginia and Rice University.

He is the author of numerous Tibetan texts, including the thirteen-volume Tibetan *Bibliographical Dictionary*, a classic reference work in the field. During the 1960s he spent ten years in Japan teaching at several of the major universities in that country—most notably, those of Tokyo and Kyoto. He is known in the English-speaking world for his *Tantric Practice in Nyingma*, a commentary on *The Words of My Perfect Teacher*, which was translated by Jeffrey Hopkins and edited by Anne Klein. His commentary on the first of Mipham Rinpoche's three *Cycles on Fundamental Mind* (*gNyug sems 'khor sums*) is now available, along with a translation of Mipham's own text, as *Fundamental Mind*, translated by Jeffrey Hopkins (Ithaca, NY: Snow Lion Publications, 2006).

Tulku Thondup Rinpoche, Cambridge, Massachusetts, and Tibet

Student of the Dodrupchen Rinpoches and incarnation of Lushül Khenpo Könchog Drönme (1859–1936), one of the four great khenpos of Dodrupchen Monastery and a student of Patrul Rinpoche, he is the well-known author of numerous essential books on the *Longchen Nyingthig*, especially his anthology of Longchenpa's writings, *The Practice of Dzogchen* (Snow Lion Publications), as well as the best-selling *The Healing Power of Mind: Simple Meditation Exercises for Health, Well-Being, and Enlightenment*, which has been translated into twelve languages. In addition he has gathered wide audiences for *Boundless Healing* and the more recent *Peaceful Death, Joyful Rebirth*, edited by Harold Talbott (all from Shambhala Publications). His website offers his teaching schedule, including workshops on these writings. Tulku's ability to draw from traditional Buddhist transmissions and bring them into play with contemporary sensibilities is one of his many remarkable gifts.

Anne Carolyn Klein (Rigzin Drolma), Ph.D., Houston, Texas

Anne Klein is a practicing student in this lineage since 1974, a founding director and resident teacher of Dawn Mountain, a center for contemplative study and practice in Houston, and Professor of Religious Studies at Rice University. She teaches foundational and other contemplative practices widely, including "Buddhism in the Body" programs, linking these traditional Tibetan practices with body-centered energy awareness. Her teaching draws on all three of the five Tibetan traditions in which she has studied, practiced, and translated texts along with having received extensive oral transmission.

She is also the author of five books, all of them exploring the relationship between effortful thinking and the release of nonconceptual wisdom: *Meeting the Great Bliss Queen* (Beacon Press; reprinted, Snow Lion Publications) *Path to the Middle: Oral Mādhyamika Philosophy in Tibet* (SUNY Press); *Knowledge & Liberation* (Snow Lion Publications), which was translated into Chinese for publication by Hong Kong University; *Knowing, Naming, and Negation* (Snow Lion Publications); and most recently, *Unbounded Wholeness: Dzogchen, Bön, and the Logic of the Nonconceptual*, co-authored with Geshe Tenzin Wangyal Rinpoche (Oxford University Press).

For more information about our ongoing programs in this tradition:
www.dawnmountain.org
info@dawnmountain.org
(713) 630-0354

May there be a grand and growing new temple,
A great stable seat for the entire lineage of the highest (Ati) practices,
A place for learning of many kinds.
Once it extends throughout the vast world,
May there be male and female yogis
In all lands everywhere, who practice and further the teachings there.
—Khetsun Sangpo Rinpoche

A prayer for Dawn Mountain and the flourishing of the Dharma, inspired and composed in Houston on September 15, 2003, at dawn.

Photos

These photos can be found in color at www.shambhala.com/heart-essence-images.

Land Images

Above and below left: Views of Tso Pema/Rewalsar Lake seen en route to Cave Retreat (currently presided over by Lama Wangdor) in Mandi, India. Traditionally known as Sahor, this is where Guru Rinpoche met Princess Mandāravā, whose father, the king, attempted to burn him in a huge pyre, which Guru Rinpoche then transformed into the lake now known as Rewalsar. Below right: Guru Rinpoche footprint outside cave above Rewalsar Lake

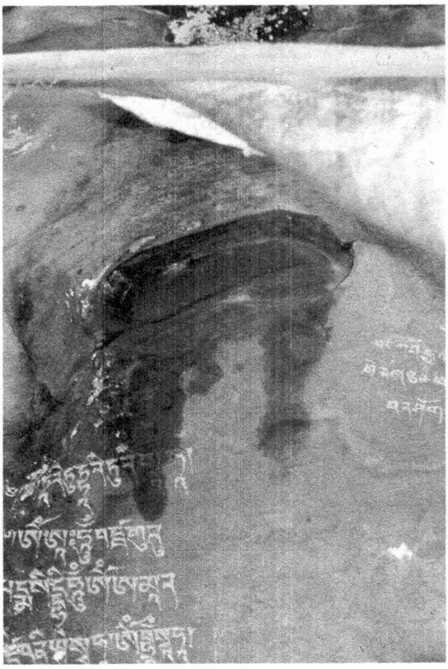

Top of stupa at Boudhanath, Nepal

Khetsun Sangpo Rinpoche speaking at the Great Stupa, Boudhanath, Nepal

Zha Temple of Uru Province, built by Vimalamitra's student and restored by Longchenpa (photo courtesy of Sharon Jackson)

View from lower Samye-Chimphu (also known as Chimphu)

Copper Mountain at Chimphu

View from Longchenpa's cave
(photo courtesy of Deb Bouvier)

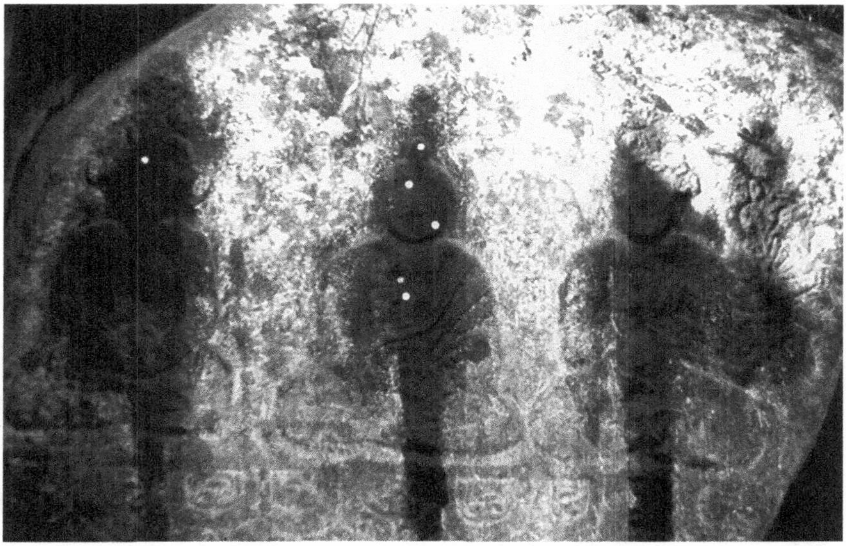

Buddhas of the three times, self-arisen at Chimphu, below Longchenpa Stupa

Self-arisen likeness of the Third Karmapa in Chimphu cave

Hill with thousands of prayer flags, Kham

Tibet's Soul-Lake, Yamdro Tso

Longchen Rabjam's Stupa at Samye Chimphu

Samye roof, rebuilt 1988

Longchenpa's meditation cave (photo courtesy of Deb Bouvier)

Jigme Lingpa Secret Flower Cave, Chimphu (photo courtesy of Deb Bouvier)

Steps to Jigme Lingpa's/
Longchenpa's Flower Cave

Inside Jigling cave (photo courtesy of Deb Bouvier)

Inside Jigme Lingpa Cave, Chimphu (photos courtesy of Deb Bouvier)

On the way to Tsogyal Soul-Lake

Above left: Tsogyal Soul-Lake

Above right: Heart-shaped sand above Yeshe Tsogyal's birthplace

Yeshe Tsogyal's birthplace: An oasis

On the way to Tsogyal Lake

Yeshe Tsogyal footprint

Transmission: Lamas

Geshe Wangyal
(photo courtesy of Katrina Thomas)

Geshe Wangyal,
Maitreya Festival

Khetsun Sangpo Rinpoche, 1974
(photo courtesy of John Buescher)

Tulku Jigme with Khetsun Sangpo Rinpoche, 2004

Lama Gompo Tsayden at his Amdo Monastery (photo courtesy of Nina Egert)

Chogyal Namkhai Norbu Rinpoche, Lhasa, circa 1987

Thrulzhig Rinpoche
(photo courtesy of
Harvey Aronson)

Tulku Thondup

Images for Meditation

Buddha, "The Jowo" (Jokhang)

Guru Rinpoche (Padmasambhava) in posture of royal ease

Great Bliss Queen, detail from painting by Lama Gompo Tsayden

Tara, ancient statue at Atisha's "Tara Temple," Lhasa

Vimalamitra

Vajrasattva

Longchenpa, painting at Kangri Thögar (photo courtesy of Deb Bouvier)

Jigme Lingpa, painting at Longchenpa's hermitage (photo courtesy of Deb Bouvier)

Jetsun Shugsep statue, main shrine room, Shugsep Nunnery

Recent Lineage through Adzom Drukpa

Adzom Gar

Tulku Gyurme Tsering (center),
at the Adzom Gesar Festival
(photographer unknown)

Mani stone, Adzom Gar

Artist monks painting main temple at Adzom Gar under the direction of Adzom Rinpoche

Statues at Adzom Gar, made by Pema Wangyal

Enshrined head of Chime Wangmo, former life of
Jetsun Khachö Wangmo, at Adzom Gar

Bone in shape of Dorje Chang from the heart of Pema Wangyal
(photo courtesy of Jetsunma)

Approaching Eight Heruka (bKa' brgyad) High Pass, heading into Ganse

Karma Benzra
(photographer unknown)

Adzom Drukpa,
Druktrul Rinpoche
(d. 2001)
(photographer unknown)

Adzom Drukpa,
Druktrul Rinpoche
(photographer unknown)

Adzom Rinpoche
in cave of Vimalamitra
Wu Tai Shan, 1999

Jetsun Kachö Wangmo, giving initiation (photo courtesy of Daniel Donner

Adzom Rinpoche teaching

Guide to the Refuge Tree Painting

THE REFUGE TREE (see p. v) was painted under the direct supervision of Lama Gonpo Tsayden of Amdo. It was photographed and digitized by Larry Shaw. While in many respects a traditional *Heart Essence* thangka, it has certain unique features and is included here as part of the personal transmission of this book. Many thanks to Ang Tsherin Sherpa, a master thangka painter now living in Oakland, California, and to his father, the renowned painter Urgen Dorje of Kathmandu, for helping us identify these figures. Most of these lamas are described by Tulku Thondup in *Masters of Meditation and Miracles*.*

Across the top

Representatives of the five buddha families and, to the far right, Green Tara

Directly above the central figures

Top: Samantabhadra and Samantabhadrī
Second: Vajrasattva
Third: Garab Dorje
Fourth: Guru Rinpoche
Fifth: Yeshe Tsogyal

* Many of these figures are associated with a cardinal direction (north, south, east, west, or center), and each direction is associated with a particular color: north with green, south with yellow, east with white, west with red, and center with blue. To simplify the guide, only the color is listed.

Lineage lamas on the left side

Top Left: (single figure) Kumarāja
Middle left: (yogi with right arm raised and red sash) Dupe Wangchuk Yeshe Dorje
Middle right: (wearing red lama hat) Kayshing Dukna Kunzang Shenpen
Bottom left: (pandita hat) Ogyen Jigme Chöki Wangpo
Bottom middle: (lotus hat) Dzogden Tulku Ngeden Tenzin Sangpo
Bottom right: (hair in top knot) Dilgo Khyentse Rinpoche

Lineage lamas on the right side

Top right: (hair in top knot) Drub Thob Mey Löpa Dorje
Middle left: (pandita hat, right arm in lap) Gyalwe Nyugu
Middle right: (pandita hat, right arm extended, palm up) Jamyang Khyentse Wangpo
Bottom left: (yogi with right arm raised) Adzom Drukpa, Drodul Pawo Dorje
Bottom center: (pandita hat, right arm bent) Dodrup Jigme Tempe Nyima (Dodrupchen III)
Bottom right: (pandita hat, arms crossed over chest) Tso Patrul (Lama Gonpo's teacher,* one of three tulkus of Dza Patrul Rinpoche, composer of *Words of My Perfect Teacher*)

The central figures

Guru Rinpoche with Yeshe Tsogyal

To their right are the eight bodhisattvas;† to their left, the eight arhats, namely, the hearers and solitary realizers such as Shariputra. Behind Guru Rinpoche are volumes of the teaching, the dharma jewel.

First row of larger figures just below Guru Rinpoche, left to right‡

Rahula, Guru Dragpo or Vajrasadhu, Avalokiteshvara (literally, Great Compassion-

* Tso Patrul Kunzang Shenpen Ozer.

† Mañjuśrī, Kṣitigarbha, Sarvanīvaraṇaviṣkambhin, Avalokiteśvara, Vajrapāṇi, Maitreya, Samantabhadra, Akaśagarbha. Another source identified these in this thangka as the eight apsaras.

‡ Rahula and so forth in Tibetan: ར་ཧུ་ལ། གུ་རུ་དྲག་པོ། ཐུགས་རྗེ་ཆེན་པོ། དཔལ་ཆེན་རྒྱས་པ། ཡུམ་ཀ་བདེ་ཆེན་རྒྱལ་མོ། སེང་གེ་གདོང་མ།

ate One),* Belchen Gyepa, Dechen Gyalmo (the Great Bliss Queen), Sinhamukha (Lion-Faced Lady)†

Second row of figures (yidams), left to center‡

Vow Holder Dorje Lekpa (a protector, with hat), Rigzin Yab Yum, Yidam Lord of Death (yellow), Yidam Yangdag (Actual Yidam, white), Belchen Dudpa (Glorious Constellation [of good qualities], blue)

Second row of figures (yidams), center to right §

Damtrin Marpo (Red-Horse-Headed, red), Dorje Shonu (Youthful Vajra, green), Southeast Yidam, Dragdul (Fierce Tamer), Tsheringma (a protector)

Middle of the third row

The three buddhas of the past, present, and future

Third row of figures, left to center

The five heroes with consorts:¶ green, red, yellow, white, blue.

* The four-armed standing Avalokiteshvara is known as Naturally Freed Suffering, Dungel Rangdrol (*sDug bsngal rang grol*). Guru Rinpoche, Avalokiteshvara, and the Great Bliss Queen are the three sources, the guru, deva, and dakini of the Longchen Nyingthig. Throughout, the guide gives whichever name, Sanskrit or Tibetan, is likely to be most familiar and provides the other name in the notes.

† Senge Dongma

‡ This row in Tibetan: དམ་ཅན་རྡོ་རྗེ་ལེགས་པ། རིགས་འཛིན་ཡབ་ཡུམ། ཡི་དམ་གཤིན་རྗེ། དཔལ་ཆེན་སྡུད་པ།

§ This row in Tibetan: རྟ་མགྲིན་དམར་པོ། རྡོ་རྗེ་གཞོན་ནུ། ཤར་ལྷོ་ཡི་དམ། ཁྲག་འདུལ [or possibly དྲག་འདུལ] ། ཚེ་རིང་མ།

¶ དཔལ་ཡབ་ཡུམ་ལྔ།

Third row of figures, center to right

The five families of dakinis:[*] green, red, yellow, white, blue.

Bottom row (protectors), left to center[†]

Raksha Karma Maning, Gonpo Peng (Protector with Staff), Shinje (Lord of Death, blue), Gonpo Ta Shon (Tiger-Riding Protector, red), Gonpo Chadrug (Six-Armed Protector, green)

Bottom row (protectors), center to right[‡]

Belden Ekazati (Glorious Ekazati), Mag Zorma,[§] Mother Who Overwhelms Harm,[¶] Dongyal (Victorious Teacher), Kungyal (All Conquering), Durthro Hlamo (Goddess of the Charnel Ground, red), Yudronma (Turquoise-Lamp Lady)

In addition, readers might wish to refer to the black and white refuge tree on p. 170 of *Words of My Perfect Teacher*. It also appears on p. 135 of Tulku Thondup's *The Tantric Tradition of the Nyingmapa* (Buddhayana, 1984).

Further, Tulku Thondup made the following key for a Longchen Nyingthig refuge tree of Dilgo Khyentse Rinpoche, which is reproduced here by permission. This refuge tree is not pictured in these pages, but is widely available. Students should be aware that different transmission lineages enrich the tradition as a whole with their own inspired variations. Any of those mentioned here can be used to guide one's visualization.

* རིགས་ལྔ་མཁའ་འགྲོ།

† This row in Tibetan: ཀར་མ་མ་ཉིང་། མགོན་པེང་། གཤིན་རྗེ། མགོན་པོ་སྟག་ཞོན། མགོན་པོ་ཕྱག་དྲུག།

‡ This row in Tibetan: དཔལ་ལྡན་ཨེ་ཀ་ཛ་ཏི། མག་ཟོར་མ། གནོད་སྦྱིན་མ། གདོང་རྒྱལ། ཀུན་རྒྱལ། དུར་ཁྲོད་ལྷ་མོ། གཡུ་སྒྲོན་མ།

§ She is virtually identical with Belden Hlamo, the protectress of Tibet. She rides a mule. Next to her, Dongyal rides a camel and Kungyal rides a deer.

¶ Apparently an epithet of the sun.

Refuge Tree of Longchen Nyingthig

As Instructed by Kyabje Dilgo Khyentse Rinpoche

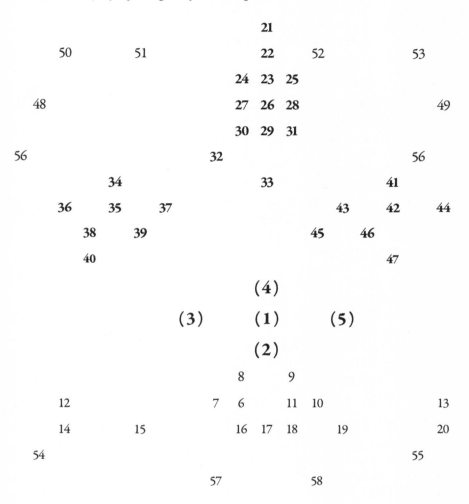

21

50 51 **22** 52 53

24 23 25

48 **27 26 28** 49

30 29 31

56 **32** 56

34 **33** **41**

36 35 37 **43 42 44**

38 39 **45 46**

40 **47**

(4)

(3) (1) (5)

(2)

8 9

12 7 6 11 10 13

14 15 16 17 18 19 20

54 55

57 58

1. Center: Guru Rinpoche and Yeshe Tsogyal
2. Front: Buddhas of the three times
3. Right: Eight Bodhisattvas (Mahayana Sangha)
4. Back: Scriptures (Dharma)
5. Left: Shravaka Monks (Theravadin Sangha)

Center: Tutelary Deities (Yi-Dam)

6. Chechog (Mahottara-heruka or Vajramahaheruka)
7. Yangdag (Shriheruka)
8. Shinje (Yamantaka)
9. Tadrin (Hayagriva)
10. Phurpa (Vajrakila)
11. Yumka, Dechen Gyalmo
12. Thugje Chenpo Dukngal Rangtrol (Avalokiteshvara)
13. Takhyung Barwa (Wrathful form of Guru Rinpoche)

Dharmapalas

14. Tsheringma
15. gZa' (Rahu)
16. Gonpo (Natha)
17. Ekazati (Ekajati)
18. Damchen Dorjelegpa (Vajrasadhu)
19. Durthrod Dagmo (Chitipati)
20. Dorje Yudronma

Lineage Teachers Before Jigme Lingpa

21. Kuntu Zangpo (Samantabhadra)
22. Dorje Sempa (Vajrasattva)
23. Garab Dorje (Prahevajra)
24. Shrisimha
25. Manjushrimitra
26. Padmasambhava
27. Jnanasutra
28. Vimalamitra
29. Yeshe Tsogyal
30. Bairotsana
31. King Thrisong Deutsen
32. Kunkhyen, Longchen Rabjam (1308–1363)
33. Rigdzin, Jigme Lingpa (1729–1798)

Lineage Lamas, after Jigme Lingpa

At the right corner of the Tree

34. First Dodrupchen, Jigme Thrinle Özer (1745–1821)
35. Do Khyentse, Yeshe Dorje (1800–1866)
36. Gyalse, Zhenphen Thaye (1800–?)
37. Patrul Rinpoche, Jigme Chökyi Wangpo (1808–1887)
38. Nyoshul, Lungtok Tenpe Nyima (1829–1901)
39. Onpo, Tendzin Norbu
40. Kathog Khenpo, Ngawang Palzang (1879–1941)

At the left corner of the Tree

41. Jigme Gyalwe Nyuku (1765–1843)
42. Jamyang Khyentse Wangpo, Dorje Zijid (1820–1892)
43. Third Dodrupchen, Jigme Tenpe Nyima (1865–1926)
44. Adzom Drugpa, Drodul Pawo Dorje (1842–1924)*
45. Dzongsar Khyentse, Chökyi Lodrö (1893–1959)*
46. Fifth Dzogchen Rinpoche, Thubten Chökyi Dorje (1872–1935)*
47. Dzogchen Khenpo, Pema Losal*

Other Tutelary Deities

48. Vajrasattva (Ngensong Jonga)
49. Vajraheruka (Ngensong Jongwa)
50. Mi-thrugpa (Akshobhya)
51. Öpagme (Amitabha)
52. Nampar Nangdze (Vairochana)
53. Menkyi Lama (Bhaishajyaguru, Medicine Buddha)
54. Drolma (Tara)

Dharmapala of Wealth

55. Namthöse (Vaishravana)

Offering Devotees

56. Offering Dakinis
57. Monk devotee
58. Lay devotee

*** These are teachers who, in person, transmitted Longchen Nyingthig teachings to Kyabje Dilgo Khyentse Rinpoche (1910–1991).**

Notes

1. The three divisions of Dzogchen teaching are the Mind, Instructional, and Spacious Dimension teachings (*sems sde, klong sde,* and *man ngag sde*). For Jigme Lingpa's statement quoted here, see *Kun mkhyen zhal lung, Nyingthig rtsa pod,* volume *hum,* folios 12a/6: *Klong ch'en po'i mkha'/ sNying ch'en po'i tig.* Thanks to Tulku Thondup for this reference.

2. Vajradhara is the resplendent (*sambhogakāya*) form of Samantabhadra, who is the *dharmakāya*. See, for example, Dudjom Rinpoche 1991, 32b.1, p. 64.

3. An earlier version of this introduction appeared in the Winter 2003 issue of *Buddhadharma*.

4. Adzom Drukpa 1976, 143.1–2. Adzom Drukpa's (A-'dzoms 'brug-pa 'Gro bdul dpa' bo rdo rje) *Thar lam gsal byed* is a commentary on the *Longchen Nyingthig Foundational Practices*. He cites here Candrakirti's *Seventy Verses on Refuge* (*skyabs 'gro bdun cu pa*; Skt. *Triśaraṇasaptati*). T3971.

5. Unnamed sutra cited by Adzom Drukpa 1976, 145.4.

6. Action, Performance, and Yoga Tantras.

7. Adzom Drukpa 1976, 147.3.

8. Some traditions touch at the heart only once, after the crown and the throat.

9. For an elaborate philosophical discussion of unbounded wholeness in Dzogchen, taken from the Bön tradition and also applicable here, see Klein and Wangyal Rinpoche 2006.

10. *Sambhogakāya.*

11. That is, I cultivate the strong sense that I will never repeat these deeds, even at the cost of my life.

12. Explicit and implicit principles upon which such understanding is based will be a focus of the book currently in preparation by Klein, Pay, and Milun, provisionally titled *The Knowing Body.*

13. Jigme Lingpa, *Collected Works*, vol. 8, pp. 861–903.

14. Jigme Lingpa, *Collected Works*, vol. 8, pp. 905–43.

15. Jigme Lingpa, Dilgo Khyentse edition, vol. *hum*, p. 647.

16. Jigme Lingpa, Dilgo Khyentse edition, vol. *om*, p. 133.

17. This appears in the *kLong snying 'don ch'a pod gnyis pa nyer mkho skor* under the title *kLong chen snying tig gi sngon 'gro'i ngag 'don rnam mkhyen lam bzang gsal byed bchas*, pp. 5–50. Patrul Rinpoche's text is also found in the second volume of the *'don ch'a* or daily prayer books published by Dodrupchen Rinpoche in Sikkhim. Thanks to Tulku Thondup on this point.

18. Thondup 1999, p. 202.

19. See ibid., p. 215ff.

20. Dudjom Rinpoche's own root teacher, Gyurme Ngreton Wangpo, was also a student of Jamyang Khyentse Wangpo.

21. Sogyal Rinpoche's worldwide Rigpa centers, the Seminary and other training centers in the lineage of the late Trungpa Rinpoche, and the many centers of the late Chagdud Rinpoche, as well as renowned Tibetan lamas such as Dodrupchen Rinpoche, Dungsei Thinley Norbu Rinpoche, Gyatrul Rinpoche, Khyentse Norbu Rinpoche, Chögyal Namkhai Norbu Rinpoche, Tulku Sang Ngag, Tulku Thondup, and Tsoknyi Rinpoche, and non-Tibetan teachers such as Lama Surya Das are among the Tibetan Buddhist communities and lamas in the West for whom the *Heart Essence* lineage and its foundational practices are central or significant. Please see page 164 regarding Dawn Mountain and its related centers' offerings in this tradition.

22. Described by Khetsun Sangpo Rinpoche in Sangpo 1982. Most Tibetan practice sessions begin with some version of this nine-fold breathing exercise. Here women and men do this practice in the very same way. Khetsun Sangpo Rinpoche, Tulku Thondup, private communication with the author.

23. *Ngag byin gyis rlab pa.* This practice, described in Sangpo 1982, pp. 197–98, can be done here, or immediately upon waking in the morning. The verses for this practice are found at the beginning of the *rNam khyen lam gsal byed* by Jamyang Khyentse Wangpo (1820–92). It is widely believed that the sixteen vowels and thirty-four consonants of the Sanskrit language have great power. Ritual recitation of these sounds is used to purify the speech in numerous contexts, especially to magnify the power of speech before extended mantra recitation (*sadhana*), and in connection with mantra retreats (*bsnyan tshams*). The vajra speech of the buddhas is embodied as Amitabha Buddha. The vowels, symbolizing wisdom, are white; the consonants, symbolizing skillful means, are red. As Khetsun Sangpo taught this practice, these form a circle around the tongue-vajra. As Tulku Thondup teaches it, the red and white syllables circle around like snakes in the hollow space of the round center of the tongue vajra. In both cases, these are surrounded by the syllables of the Mantra

of Interdependent Causation, *YE DHARMA HETU*, etc. Here that mantra is imagined as a rosary of blue or yellow pearls.

In addition, Bön traditions maintain that each line of the alphabet promotes health in specific parts of the body—for example, *GA KHA KA NGA* in the throat, *HA A* in the stomach, and so on.

24. That is, the Tathagata taught that all suffering arises from causes, and he taught how to cease such suffering through practice of the path. This phrase, "the heart of dependent arising" can be seen as condensing the Four Noble Truths and is regarded as the pith of Buddha's teaching. It is found in Sanskrit scriptures telling of of Shariputra's conversion. The newly ordained Shariputra tells a senior monk, the Ven. Asvajit, "Monk, all I need is the gist. What is the need for many elaborations. Tell me the gist." Ven. Asvajit recited this verse and Shariputra's wisdom eye immediately opened to the nature of things. *Catusparisatasutra*, translated in John Strong, *The Experience of Buddhism* (Belmont, CA: Wadsworth, 1994), p. 53.

25. These, as well as the eight incompatible inclinations that follow, are discussed by Longchen Rabjam in his *Wish-Granting Treasury* (*Yi bzhin mdzod*). See also *Words*, pp. 29–33, or Sangpo 1982, pp. 48–52.

26. *bdud kyis zin*. For example, Angulimala was in the thrall of a teacher who told him the way to liberation was to kill one thousand persons and collect their fingers. Sangpo 1982, p. 49.

27. These refer to powerful, habitual disinclinations to practice, so strong and obscuring that they virtually obstruct any possibility for cultivation. These counter-inclinations do not refer merely to occasional missteps in one's practice.

28. Thanks to Tulku Thondup for this gloss. Literally, one could also read this as "extreme wrong [view]."

29. *tam tshigs*. These are special pledges or promises associated with Tantric initiations.

30. The weapons, hammers, saws, and room are all molten red hot iron as well.

31. This phrase is included in the Tibetan text published by Tulku Thondup under the title *The "Excellent Path of Omniscience" of Kun Khyen Jig-Med Ling-pa* and translated by him (Shantiniketan, 1979).

32. This is, famously, one of the richest teaching verses of the text. Numerous commentaries have been written on it and some variant interpretations. The translation here accords with the commentary of Yukhok Chatralwa Choying Rangdrol (1872–1952), which accords also with Khetsun Sangpo's and Adzom Rinpoche's explanations in teaching. Tulku Thondup's consultation was also important here.

33. Grammatically, it is possible to interpret *sugata* as a gloss on "Three Real Jewels"—that is, as referring to Buddha, Dharma, and Sangha, as suggested by Tulku Thondup's translation (1982:9) and rendered here. It is also possible to understand this verse to mean that guru, deva, and dakini are the composite of all *sugatas* just

as are the lama, deity, and dakini, as Khetsun Sangpo Rinpoche (1982:119–20) comments. This interpretation is reflected in the chantable translation.

34. Guru, yidam (most intimate deity), and dakini.

35. Tib. *rtsa, rlung, thigle*; Skt. *nādi, prāna, bindu.*

36. That is, I cultivate the strong sense that I will never repeat these deeds, even at the cost of my life.

37. *shon nu bum ba'i sku.* Literally, "youthful vase dimension," signifying the primordial buddha now present deep within the obscuring vessel of the body.

38. See Patrul 1994:297–307; or Sangpo 161–66.

39. Tromo is a fierce black female deity.

40. Classically, the four *bdud* named in Severance (and elsewhere) are (1) the aggregate fiend (*phung po bdud*), (2) the affliction fiend (*nyon mongs pa'i bdud*), (3) the lord of death fiend (*'chi bdag gi bdud*), and (4) the divine child fiend (*lha'i bu'i bdud*). These "fiends" typically signify what we would call emotions. For example, the divine child fiend is associated with distraction.

    In Anuyoga, the seventh of the nine vehicles, five *bdud* are listed, according to the *Treasure of All-Pervasive Knowing* (*Shes bya kun khyab mdzod*) by Jamgon Kongtrul, vol. 2, p. 192. These are: (1) the demon that causes insecurity through divisive thoughts, (2) the demon that is laziness with respect to the equanimity of the real, (3) the demon that is capricious with respect to pleasure and social diversions, (4) the demon of the sharp sword of harsh speech, and (5) the demon that causes disturbances in a wrathful, fierce manner. From the Rangjung Yeshe dictionary.

41. *kāya* (Tib. *sku*). The three dimensions, or bodies, of a buddha.

42. Lama Gonpo Tsayden suggests repeating this prayer three times and reciting one hundred mantras after each repetition of this verse. When you have the time, please consider this as a way of adding power to your practice. Tulku Thondup notes that if you are doing the guru yoga part, briefly or as a daily practice, then you do not need to recite the mantras between the prayer verses but only at the end (before the lineage prayers preceding the four initiations).

43. *Commentary* glosses *skal ba* as *sa bon*, or "seed" (143, last line).

44. *Commentary*, 144.3–4.

45. The *caṇḍālī* is the source of all bodily warmth and is located within the central channel, four fingerwidths below the navel. Sangpo 1982:177.

46. *Commentary*, 144.11–12.

47. *Commentary*, 145.2–3.

48. These instructions, not explicit in Khetsun Sangpo Rinpoche's commentary, are found in the material from Lama Gonpo and in Tulku Thondup.

49. These instructions, which do not appear in the Tibetan text, are given by Khetsun Sangpo Rinpoche, following Patrul Rinpoche. See also *Commentary*, 147.1–3.

50. The verse in Dodrupchen's text requests the lama to reside in the lotus at the crown. Our Tibetan recitation text (n.p.) reads "heart" rather than "crown" at this juncture, and Khetsun Sangpo Rinpoche also taught the practice in this way. Tulku Thondup has elaborated as follows: "As you go to sleep, see the lama descending through your central channel to sit in your heart, which is shaped as a lotus of light. Your entire body fills with light (unless this makes sleeping difficult). Enter sleep within an awareness of this luminous clarity. If possible, feel that your light touches the entire universe, which melts into light and merges into yourself. You then merge with the lama at your heart and dissolve into emptiness, thereafter remaining in naked union with awareness and emptiness."

51. *Commentary*, 148.3–7.

52. Some recensions of the Tibetan text, such as that published by Tulku Thondup, do not include the purification of speech practice that follows; like the instructions on purifying the breath, in some cases this remains simply part of the oral tradition, which is integral to the practice transmission.

53. A reference to the mantra of dependent arising, for *rten 'grel*, or dependent arising, can also be understood as an omen, or indication, of that which will occur in dependence on what is happening now.

54. The buddhas' heirs are bodhisattvas.

55. Most generally, *siddhis* are the powers, accomplishments, and wisdom arising from practice.

56. In this line, vowels with long diacritical marks are held for two beats; vowels without, for one beat. In the course of the Sanskrit alphabet recitation as a whole, sounds move from the chest (locus of *A*) up to the throat (*KA, KHA* ...), to the palate (*CHA, CHHA* ...), to mid-palate (*ṬA, ṬHA, ḌA* ...), to the teeth (*TA, THA* Ö), then to lips touching (*PA, PHA* Ö), and finally, to lips open (*YA, RA, LA, WA*).

57. These sounds are retroflex, meaning that the tongue curves back on itself, touching the top of the palate, when pronouncing them.

58. These sounds are dentals, pronounced with the tongue touching the back of the top teeth.

59. This phrase, "the heart of dependent arising" is regarded as the pith of Buddha's teaching. It is found in Sanskrit scriptures telling of of Shariputra's conversion. The newly ordained Shariputra tells a senior monk, "Monk, all I need is the gist. What is the need for many elaborations. Tell me the gist." His mentor, Ven. Ashvajit, recites this verse, and Shariputra's wisdom eye immediately opens to the nature of reality. *Catusparisatasutra* translated in John Strong, *The Experience of Buddhism* (Belmont, CA: Wadsworth, 1994), p. 53.

60. Poetic license has been taken in rendering *dran pa* and *shes bzhin*, which are

frequently translated as "mindfulness" and "introspection." Tulku Thondup notes, in accordance with the instructions of Yukhok Chatralwa Choying Rangdrol (1872–1952), that this prayer calls forth both the external lama, the being imagined to move from one's heart to one's crown, and the internal lama, which is mindfulness and awareness. The remainder of the prayers, up to the refuge verse, are addressed to the lama at one's crown, a unification of Guru Rinpoche, Longchen Rabjam, Jigme Lingpa, and one's own root teachers. As much as possible, one maintains the sense that the guru resides there throughout the day.

When we engage in the subsequent visualizations, we may lose direct connection with the lama at our crown, but we should not think that this connection has necessarily disappeared. Many deities, or a single deity in many forms, can be present in the same place. There are no limits in this dimension. Even when we dissolve one deity before visualizing another, as when we move from visualizing the Refuge Tree to the practice of Vajrasattva, even though one becomes invisible, it has not necessarily completely gone. Tulku Thondup.

61. These are "common" in the sense that they are shared with the practitioners of Nikāya (or Theravādan) Buddhism.

62. The following verses frame the four thoughts that turn our minds to practice: (1) appreciation of the specific qualities of a precious human life that bring freedom to practice, (2) life's impermanence, (3) karma, and (4) the suffering of cyclic existence.

63. Such beings have no discrimination, thus no possibility for sacred practice.

64. Refers to Guru Rinpoche.

65. *blo sna* literally means "attitude," or "frame of mind." Since this is what one identifies with most strongly, and to avoid the mistaken notion that practice is about mind as we ordinarily conceive it, I have taken poetic license and simply say "me" instead of "my mind" here.

66. Today we understand that both Longchenpa and Jigme Lingpa are the omniscient lamas who are "all knowing." When Jigme Lingpa himself wrote these lines, he meant the phrase "all knowing" to invoke Longchenpa. For his own students, the "Kind Lama" of the third line signified Jigme Lingpa himself. Subsequent generations, including ourselves, understand the third line to refer to our own teacher.

67. Here, "these ones" refers to Longchenpa and Jigme Lingpa.

68. These refer to powerful, habitual disinclinations to practice, so strong and obscuring that they virtually obstruct any possibility for cultivation. These counter-inclinations do not refer merely to occasional missteps.

69. *tam tshigs*. These are special pledges or promises associated with Tantric initiations.

70. The *bardo* is the intermediate state between death and the next life.

71. *Wangs* (*dbang*) are initiations, or empowerments. The four *wangs* are: vase, secret, wisdom, and word. See the "Guru Yoga" recitation section (pp. 50–52, 77–80) and the Guru Yoga chapters in Patrul 1994 or Sangpo 1982.

72. This can connote crude, improper, or unpredictable behavior or, alternatively, senseless babble.

73. Literally, "though meditation is distracted" (*sgom pa yengs*).

74. The text specifically mentions pilgrimage, which can be a worthy religious activity but may also become a form of amusement. Meditation is more highly praised for practitioners.

75. A reference to the eight worldly dharmas (*'jig rten chos brgyad*) of being overly affected, positively or negatively, by: gain, loss, fame, ill repute, praise, blame, pleasure, pain.

76. Here "uncommon" refers to practices unique to the Mahayana.

77. Khetsun Sangpo Rinpoche explains that the *sugatas* are the composite of the three roots (guru, deity, and dakini).

78. "Full" refers to enlightenment replete with all good qualities.

79. *Sambhogakāya*.

80. That is, I cultivate the strong sense that I will never repeat these deeds, even at the cost of my life.

81. *yab yum*, "male and female."

82. Chögyi Dragpa 113:7 notes that one calls here for protection just as a child calls for its mother.

83. This refers to a *cakravārtin*, i.e., the emanation dimension.

84. This refers to the five inalienable, or definite, attributes, which are: (1) place: Richly Ornate Pure Land (*Akanishta*; *'Og min stug po bkod*); (2) teacher: Vairochana Gangchentso (*rnam snang gangs chen mtsho*); (3) retinue: tenth-ground bodhisattvas; (4) teaching: Mahayana; and (5) time: "continuous wheel of eternity" (*rtag pa rgyun gyi bskor ba*).

85. This refers to the *sambhogakāya*, or resplendent dimension.

86. *shon nu bum ba'i sku*. Literally, youthful vase dimension, signifying the primordial buddha now present deep within the obscuring vessel of the body.

87. This refers to the *dharmakāya*, or actual buddha dimension.

88. Severance is famous for overcoming the four *dü* (*bdud*), usually translated as "demons." Classically, the four *bdud* named in severance (and elsewhere) are (1) aggregate fiend (*phung po bdud*), (2) affliction fiend (*nyon mongs pa'i bdud*), (3) lord of death fiend (*'chi bdag gi bdud*), and (4) divine child fiend (*lha'i bu'i bdud*). These "fiends" typically signify what we would call emotions. For example, the divine child fiend is associated with distraction.

89. The three dimensions, or bodies, of a buddha (Skt. *kāya*, Tib. *sku*).

90. Chögyi Dragpa 125:7–10 notes that he wears the deep blue gown of a *mantrika*, the

red-yellow religious robes of a monk, the kingly maroon shawl of a king, as well as the white brocade of a bodhisattva.

91. *Pema* is the Tibetan form of *padma*, which is the Sanskrit term for "lotus." For the sake of simplicity, the term has been rendered as *pema* throughout this book.

92. Literally, "mother," referring to his female consort.

93. A *rigzin* (*rig 'dzin*) is someone who is a holder (*'dzin pa*) of open presence (*rig pa*). See Sangpo 1982, pp. 15–16; the four main categories of rigzin are described on pp. 175–79.

94. A *yidam* is a personal deity, an enlightened being into whose mandala one has been initiated.

95. *Jetsun* translates as "venerable" and is a traditional term of respect.

96. Lama Gonpo Tsayden suggests repeating this prayer three times and reciting one hundred mantras after each repetition of this verse. When you have the time, please consider this as a way of adding power to your practice. Tulku Thondup notes that if you are doing the guru yoga part, briefly or as a daily practice, then you do not need to recite the mantras between the prayer verses but only at the end (before the lineage prayers preceding the four initiations).

97. The two obstructions (*sgrib pa*) to liberation and to omniscience.

98. In the recitation text from Lama Gonpo, this prayer is recited here. In the texts of Tulku Thondup and others, this prayer follows the Becoming Vajrayogini prayer below.

99. In Sangpo 1982, in accordance with the instructions that Jeffrey Hopkins received from Khetsun Sangpo Rinpoche, this prayer to the lineage lamas is recited after the initiation. According to Tulku Thondup and in the version from Lama Gonpo, the lineage prayer precedes the initiation in this and other Tibetan recitation practices. Here, we follow this more customary order.

100. *gya ched* signifies there is no size because there is no limit, such as great or small. *phyogs lhung* signifies falling into extremes of (being set in) a particular directionality such as this or that, north or south, yours or mine.

101. Samantabhadra.

102. Vajrasattva.

103. Skt. Manjushrimitra, who is the lord of Dzogchen, which is the peak, or ninth, of the nine vehicles (*yāna*; *theg pa*).

104. Jambudvipa is the southern of the four continents surrounding Mount Meru. This is often said to be the world we live in; sometimes, however, it is associated with the continent of Asia.

105. The "heart children," or Dharma heirs, are: the king, Trisong Detsen, the student, Vairochana (sometimes also said to be the twenty-five students of Guru Rinpoche), and the friend, his consort Yeshe Tsogyal. 137:10.

106. *Khandro* (Tib. *mkha' 'gro*), literally "sky goer," is Tibetan for *dakini* (Skt).

107. Jamyang Khyentse Wangpo.

108. *shes nyams yid dpyod las 'das rig pa'i gtangs*. More literally, "the radiance of innate presence (*rig pa*), which is beyond consciousness, experience, or mental analysis," that is, beyond any activity of mind or mental fabrication.

109. Refers to the Dzogchen path of *khregs chod*, or setting free, in which one sets free all tensions and releases the bonds of thought.

110. Refers to the Dzogchen path of *thod rgal*, or soaring forth, in which one ascends the stages through vision.

111. According to Chögyi Dragpa's (142:12–13) commentary, this signifies liberation through experiencing, wearing, touching, seeing, and hearing.

112. Poetic gloss on "natural" (*rang bzhin*).

113. Emanation dimension buddha (*nirmanakāya*).

114. *skyes rim*. Sometimes translated as "the development stage," it is the first of the two levels of Tantric practice, in which one cultivates the ability to clearly sense oneself as a deity.

115. Resplendent dimension buddha (*sambhogakāya, klong sku*).

116. The *caṇḍālī* is the source of all bodily warmth and is located within the central channel, four fingerwidths below the navel. Sangpo 1982, p. 177.

117. Reference to the Copper-Colored Mountain, abode of Guru Rinpoche, here associated with the fabulous area of Nga yab (*rnga yab*). In Buddhist cosmology, the western subcontinent of Jambudvipa, also sometimes said to be northwest of Bodhgaya (depending on whether Jambu itself is considered to be our entire Earth or only the Asian continent).

118. Literally, "the Venerable Lotus-Arisen One," that is, Guru Rinpoche.

119. In the Dodrupchen transmission, as it is given in *rNam khyen lam bzang*, this prayer appears before the recitation of the *siddhi* mantra, just prior to the prayers to the lineage lamas. Here, with Khetsun Sangpo Rinpoche, we follow Patrul Rinpoche's tradition, as expounded in Patrul 1994, and Khyentse Wangpo, as expounded in his 1966.

120. Khetsun Sangpo Rinpoche, following the tradition of Adzom Drukpa, places this prayer here. The Dodrupchen, Patrul, and Khyentse recitation orders place the prayer before the initiations. We have included it in both places.

121. These instructions, which do not appear in the Tibetan text, were given by Khetsun Sangpo Rinpoche, following Patrul Rinpoche.

122. An earlier version of this narrative appeared in the *Tara Mandala Newsletter* in 2000, written at the request of founder Tsultrim Allione.

123. *Zhing sgrub.*

124. *Snang srid dbang du sdud pa'i gsol 'debs byin rlabs sprin chen bzhugs so,* "The Great Clouds of Blessings, the prayer that grants dominion over all that appears or exists," composed by Ju Mipham Rinpoche in the Earth-Hare Year, 1879. This translation benefits from the prose translations of Richard Barron (Chogyi Nyima), which is available to practitioners through the Chagdud Foundation, and the unattributed *Rigpa 2006 Calendar* version.

The Adzom Rinpoche text translation has benefited from the many generous explanations of its author over the years, for which I was sometimes the oral translator. It has also been improved in a number of places from the insight of Erik Drew, who orally translated some of these teachings as well, and from Tsultrim Allione's suggestions regarding an earlier version published by Dawn Mountain.

125. *Dharmakāya* (*chöku*), the actual buddha dimension.

126. Guhyajñāna, or "Secret Wisdom," a dakini teacher of Guru Rinpoche, revealed by the tertön Kunzang Dechen Gyalpo.

127. Cakrasamvara.

128. Rigjema (Kurukullā) is a red-golden female goddess who is a manifestation of Tara. When the Great Fifth Dalai Lama passed into nirvana while contemplating her, this was understood as an auspicious indication of his future enlightened activity, since subjugation (*dbang 'gyur*) is the special feat attained through the rites of Rigjema. Dudjom Rinpoche 1991, p. 824.

129. That is, cyclic or samsaric existence, and the peace of nirvana. Poetic license is taken in using the same term to translate *'khor 'das*, which literally means "cyclic existence and nirvana." The latter is etymologized in Tibetan as "passage beyond suffering" and, hence, the ultimate state of peace.

130. Grammatically, it is possible to interpret *sugata* as a gloss on "Three Real Jewels"—that is, as referring to Buddha, Dharma, and Sangha, as in Tulku Thondup's translation (1982:9) and as it is rendered here. It is also possible to understand this verse to mean that guru, deva, and dakini are the composite of all *sugatas* just as are the lama, deity, and dakini, as Khetsun Sangpo Rinpoche comments (1982, pp. 119–20). This interpretation is reflected in the chantable translation.

131. Tib. *rtsa, rlung, thigle*; Skt. *nādi, prāna, bindu.*

132. *thugs rjes.* The compassionate movement of outgoing energy that, with pure essence and spontaneously perfected nature, characterizes the mandala of an enlightened mind.

The lines of the refuge verse end with a Tibetan mark indicating that each line is a revealed treasure or *terma* (*gterma*); in this case, revealed from Jigme Lingpa's *Longchen Nyingthig* foundational practices.

133. The revealed treasure (*gter ma*) tradition of the *Heart Essence* lineage is unique in adding *HŪṂ PHAṬ* to the end of this mantra. The word (*bka' ma*) tradition of Jigme Lingpa's text ends the mantra with *ĀḤ.*

The Sanskrit transliteration of the mantra: *OṂ VAJRASATTVA SAMAYAM ANUPĀLAYA, VAJRASATTVA TVENOPATIṢṬHA, DṚḌO ME BHĀVA, SUTOṢNYO ME BHAVA, SUPOṢNYO ME BHĀVA, ANURAKTO ME BHĀVA, SARVA-SIDDHIṂ ME PRAYACHCHHA, SARVA-KARMASU CHA ME CITTAṂSHRIYĀṂ KURU, HŪṂ HA HA HA HA HO, BHAGAVAN-SARVA-TATHĀGATA-VAJRA, MĀ ME MUÑCHA VAJRĪ BHĀVA, MAHĀSAMAYA-SATTVA, ĀḤ HŪṂ PHAṬ.*

134. Adzom Paylo Rinpoche spoke this verse spontaneously at Kamalasila Center, in December 2004, in his room between *semtri*.

135. Often translated as "pistil," which is seen when a flower opens. *Commentary* glosses this word as "blooming." See Tulku Thondup 1995, p. 176.

136. Vowels are called *āli*; consonants, *kāli*.

137. A reference to the mantra of dependent arising, as dependent arising (*rten 'grel*) can also be understood as a cause, an omen, or an indication of that which will occur in dependence on what is happening now.

138. "Full" refers to enlightenment, i.e., replete with all good qualities.

139. Often known as the four immeasurables, these are common to both southern and northern Buddhist traditions. They are: immeasurable love, immeasurable compassion, immeasurable joy, and immeasurable equanimity.

140. *yab yum*, "father and mother."

141. *dön* (*gdon*). This refers to human and nonhumans who do harm.

142. Because it is the tradition to recite mantra as heard from one's teacher, this mantra is written here phonetically, in accordance with Tibetan pronunciation, not actual Sanskrit transcription. Most notably, the Sanskrit *vajra* is rendered *bendzra* and the Sanskrit *cha* is pronounced *tsa*.

143. Adzom Paylo Rinpoche notes that some say *MA ME* here. Either is correct.

144. The revealed treasure (*gter ma*) tradition of the *Heart Essence* lineage is unique in adding *HŪṂ PHAṬ* to the end of this mantra. The word (*bka' ma*) tradition ends the mantra with *ĀḤ*.

145. An abbreviation of Dorje Sempa, that is, Vajrasattva.

146. This is an abbreviated practice of "cutting attachment," or *chöd* (*gcod*).

147. *Wangs* (*dbang*) are initiations or empowerments.

148. See the prose translation for the identities of the individuals named in this lineage (pp. 43–44).

149. *Drib* (*sgrib pa*) are obstructions.

150. Dorje Chang is Vajradhara.

151. The five "aggregates" of body and mind: material form, feelings, perceptions, dispositions, and consciousness.

List of Audio Tracks

About the Sound Recording

These are not performances, but practices. We did our best to follow Jetsunma's lead, though she is impossible to equal, and in any case, we inevitably infused the chanting with our own cultural sensibilities. We hope you are inspired to practice as best opens your own heart. You can download these chants for free at www.shambhala.com/heartessence.

Melody revealed by Adzom Paylo Rinpoche.

Tibetan[1]

Heart Essence, the Vast Expanse (T-HE),
by Jigme Lingpa, sung by Jetsun Kacho Wangmo

1. *Great Bliss Blazing*, by Mipham Rinpoche T-GBB-1 ... 1:41
2. Purification of Speech T-HE-2 ... 1:40
3. Calling the Lama T-HE-3 ... 1:32
4. The Four Thoughts T-HE-4 ... 7:28
5. Refuge and Bodhicitta T-HE-5 ... 2:46
6. Vajrasattva T-HE-6 ... 4:14
7. Mandala T-HE-7 ... 1:23
8. Severance T-HE-8 ... 2:00

52. Purification of Winds and Speech E-WS-WO-52 .... 1:41

53. Calling the Lama and the Four Thoughts E-WS-WO-53 .. 1:57

54. Refuge and Bodhicitta E-WS-WO-54 .... 1:54

55. Vajrasattva E-WS-WO-55 .... 1:07

56. Mandala E-WS-WO-56 .... 0:27

57. Severance (Dawn Mountain Sangha) E-WS-WO-57 .... 0:24

58. Guru Yoga E-WS-WO-58 .... 3:50

59. Prayer to the Lineage Lamas E-WS-WO-59 .... 1:55

60. Sharing the Merit, Long Life Prayers,
Recitation after Meditation E-WS-WO-60 .... 2:13

61. Prayer to the *Heart Essence* Protectors E-WS-WO-61 ...... 0:50

62. Faithful Student Song E-WS-WO-62 .... 3:20

Total Time: 153:39

Practice texts for both Jigme Lingpa's *Heart Essence, the Vast Expanse* and Adzom Rinpoche's *Condensed Heart Essence* are available for download at www.dawnmountain.org. Other materials for practice will be gradually added as well. The practice texts include Tibetan, transliterated Tibetan, and English, as well as images related to the meditations. We welcome sample recordings of your own chanting and will post these for others' inspiration.

Notes

1. In ways suggestive of how various branches and monasteries of *Heart Essence* differ, Jetsunma's recording varies slightly from our text: a) she omits the final eight-line verse on p. 132, inserting its first four lines as part of the middle verse on 133; b) at the end of the sixth line from the bottom on p. 133, she sings "La" instead of "*bcas,*" both make perfect sense in Tibetan; c) she omits the next two lines on p. 133; d) she sings the third line from the bottom on p. 133 after the third line from the end of the "Prayerful Aspirations for This Life" on p. 134; e) she does not sing the last four shorter lines above the stanza break on p. 137—the same prayer also appears just before the initiation, and she sings it there; f) after the last line of Tibetan before "Dedication Prayers: Sharing the Goodness of Our Practice" on page 138, she adds three verses not in our text, then continues on with the text as written.

2. By all means listen to his version of "The Faithful Student Song" on the last track of the sound recording.